ALL-STARS OF THE NFL

Action-packed profiles of eight football superstars: Terry Bradshaw, O.J. Simpson, Bill Bergey, Ken Houston, Larry Little, Ray Guy, Isaac Curtis, and Joe Greene.

ALL-STARS OF THE NFL

BY BOB RUBIN

Illustrated with photographs

RANDOM HOUSE · NEW YORK

THE PUNT PASS AND KICK
NFL
LIBRARY

To Penny—wife, best friend, and a heck of a good typist

PHOTOGRAPH CREDITS: Vernon J. Biever, 10, 39, 50–51, 106; Clifton Boutelle, 9, 21, 34, 54, 61, 72, 102, 118, 134; Malcolm W. Emmons, 31, 82, 110, 139; United Press International, ends, 6–7, 33, 43, 48, 62–63, 66, 77, 86, 90, 97, 122, 143, 145; Wide World Photos, 16, 26, 70, 85, 98, 114, 115, 126, 130–131.

COVER: SPORTS ILLUSTRATED photograph by Heinz Kluetmeier © Time, Inc

Library of Congress Cataloging in Publication Data
Rubin, Bob.   All-stars of the NFL.   (Punt, pass & kick library)
SUMMARY: Biographical sketches of eight outstanding players from the National Football League: Bradshaw, Bergey, Guy, Houston, Little, Curtis, Greene, and Simpson.
1. Football—Biography—Juvenile literature. 2. National Football League—Biography —Juvenile literature. [1. Football—Biography. 2. National Football League] I. Title.
GV939.A1R82   796.33'2'0922 [B] [920]   76–8133
ISBN 0–394–83258–2   ISBN 0–394–93258–7 lib. bdg.

Manufactured in the United States of America   1 2 3 4 5 6 7 8 9 0

CONTENTS

ALL-STARS OF THE NFL

INTRODUCTION

Of the tens of thousands of college football players in the United States, only a relative few—1,204 to be exact—are good enough to go on to play in the National Football League. And of those 1,204, only a relative few are good enough to be called All-Stars. This book is about eight of them—the best of the best in America's toughest sport. In the chapters that follow, you will discover how these eight players became All-Stars. But first let's take a quick look at each player and the position he plays.

No position in pro football requires a greater combination of brains, leadership, and physical ability than *quarterback*. And Terry Bradshaw has them all. The quarterback is the leader of the offense. In an average game, he must call approximately 60 plays, and he has just 25 seconds to make each call. In those few seconds he must consider such factors as the type of defense his opponents are using, the score of the game, the down and the number of yards needed for a first down, the weather, the field conditions, and the individual abilities and weaknesses of his teammates and rivals.

If he has called a running play, the quarterback hands the ball off to a *running back,* who tries to pick up a first down—or, better yet, a touchdown. And when it comes to running backs, there's none greater than O.J. Simpson, who holds the NFL records for most yards gained in a single game and in a season.

If the quarterback calls for a pass play, however, he looks to a *pass receiver.* A great receiver like Isaac Curtis has the speed to outrun the fastest defenders and the concentration and sure hands to catch—and hold onto—the ball.

Good as they are, Simpson and Curtis couldn't get very far without some great blocking from their offensive linemen. A tank of a man at 6-foot-1 and 265 pounds, Larry Little is a *guard* who opens up holes in the defensive line to give the backs some running room. And on passing plays, he protects the quarterback from onrushing tacklers.

When a team can't pick up a first down, it's time for the *punter* to do his job. Ray Guy can kick long, towering punts. They hang in the air long enough to allow his teammates to get downfield and tackle the opposing receiver, thereby preventing long runbacks.

Of course, the offense is only half the story in

football. The defensive players are just as important. And the most important defender is the *middle linebacker.* Known as "the quarterback of the defense," the middle linebacker often calls the defensive alignment he and his teammates will assume on each play. His decisions are nearly as complex as those facing the quarterback on the other side of the line of scrimmage. In addition to calling defensive signals, big Bill Bergey also leads his team in tackles. He has the speed necessary to pursue the ball carrier and the sheer strength required to bring him down.

The workhorses of the defense are the defensive linemen, and there's none better than *tackle* Mean Joe Greene. Joe and the other linemen must be able to stop ball carriers coming up the middle. They must also rush the passer and range toward the sidelines on sweeps and end runs. A lineman must be big and strong enough to fight off one, two, and even three blockers.

The *safety* is part of the defensive backfield, a team's last line of defense. A safety's biggest job is defending against passes by staying with the speedy pass receivers sent out by the other team. But he must also be willing to tackle a charging ball carrier who has gotten past the other defenders. Ken Houston has the power, speed, and courage to excel at this demanding position.

Those are our eight All-Stars. Their personalities and temperaments vary as greatly as their jobs. But there are some things they all have in common—namely, the tremendous drive, determination, and talent it takes to succeed in the world of pro football.

TERRY BRADSHAW

Late in the 1971 season, ten Pittsburgh Steelers huddled and looked up expectantly at their muscular blond quarterback. The struggling Steelers, losing badly to a poor Houston Oiler team, were waiting for young Terry Bradshaw to call a play.

But Bradshaw just stared at the ground. Seconds ticked away. The silence in the huddle was deafening. The harder Bradshaw concentrated, the more confused he became.

Tension mounted in the small circle of men. A teammate snapped at Bradshaw, "Call something, darn it!" The quarterback's fair skin reddened with embarrassment, but he remained speechless. Finally, a receiver barked out a play, and the Steelers broke the long huddle.

The play was inappropriate and went nowhere. The

Steelers went nowhere for the rest of the game. (They lost to the Oilers, 29–3). Worst of all for the long-range future of the team, sophomore quarterback Terry Bradshaw appeared to be going nowhere.

Terry's rookie year had been a disaster. He'd completed just 38.1 percent of his passes, thrown only six for touchdowns, led the league in interceptions with 24, and been sacked 25 times by opposing linemen. Statistically, his second season showed some improvement. But his performance in the huddle at Houston clearly showed that he was still light-years away from mastery of his job.

Bradshaw was confused. Unsure of what he was doing on the field, he was frustrated and miserable. After almost two full years in the NFL, he couldn't seem to solve the mystery of pro football. Steeler fans booed him constantly. His coaches and teammates criticized him for his poor play-calling, lack of concentration, nervousness, and general lack of leadership.

His more sympathetic critics urged patience. They pointed out that top professional quarterbacks take time to develop. But when Bradshaw continued to struggle through his third and fourth seasons, even they joined the lynch mob. Gradually, all the criticisms of Bradshaw were combined into one catchall charge—he just wasn't smart enough to be a professional quarterback.

When Bradshaw first entered the league, however, there had been none of that kind of talk. He'd been the number one pick in the 1970 NFL draft and the most highly acclaimed quarterback prospect since Joe Namath joined the Jets five years earlier. A rock-hard

6-foot-3 and 215 pounds, Bradshaw had shown his cannonlike arm during his college career. The Pittsburgh Steelers, who'd spent 36 years in the league without winning a single championship, had seen Bradshaw as the answer to their problems.

Bradshaw was a country boy with country ways and a boyish habit of blurting out whatever was on his mind. He quickly became known as "Li'l Abner" or "Ozark Ike" to the city slickers of Pittsburgh. At first, they used the nicknames affectionately. But as the seasons passed and their hopes for a championship dimmed, the fans grew ugly. Bradshaw became "The Dummy" and his rural background became a source of ridicule.

By 1974, Bradshaw had lost his starting job with the Steelers. He had reached a crossroads in his life. Either he would fold up and quit or find some inner strength to turn his life around. A deeply religious man, Bradshaw found that strength in his faith. Midway through the season he regained his starting job. And suddenly, in one of the most dramatic turnabouts ever seen in pro football, he became the magnificent quarterback everyone always thought he could be.

Now he was in total command of the Steeler huddle. Now he called the right plays. And now his concentration was complete. Now, at last, football was again fun for Terry Bradshaw, who had first fallen in love with the game as a little boy in Shreveport, Louisiana.

Just as he was not an instant success as a professional, Bradshaw had had some rocky moments in football as a youngster. "Looking back on those childhood years, there's no doubt about it—I just wasn't very good," he admitted. "I've read biographies of professional athletes that tell about unbroken success from Pee Wee League on up. You know the type. They start by breaking all the kiddie league records, are named All-City in junior high, All-State in high school, and All-America in college, leading their teams to fame, glory, and perfect seasons along the way. They get to the pros never knowing what it feels like to be cut from the team, or even to sit on the bench. There are lots of guys like that in professional sports, but you can bet your bottom dollar I'm not one of them."

Terry was a small and skinny seventh-grader when he tried out for his junior high school football team. The coach gave a welcoming speech in which he stressed that he couldn't care less about the size of the candidates—he just wanted "winners." But then the coach proceeded to pick every big kid in the crowd.

Terry had to be content to play quarterback on a city league team. The next year the Bradshaws moved into a new school district, and Terry again went out for his junior high team. Again he and the other small boys were completely ignored when uniforms were given out. But Bradshaw had one hope this time. The coach had said that those boys who hadn't made the team could come to practice and watch.

Terry showed up at the first practice session, determined to make himself noticed. He picked up a loose ball and began to throw it on the sidelines. After he'd fired a few spirals, Terry saw the coach watching him. "I did everything I knew how to with a football and some things I had never thought of before," Terry recalled.

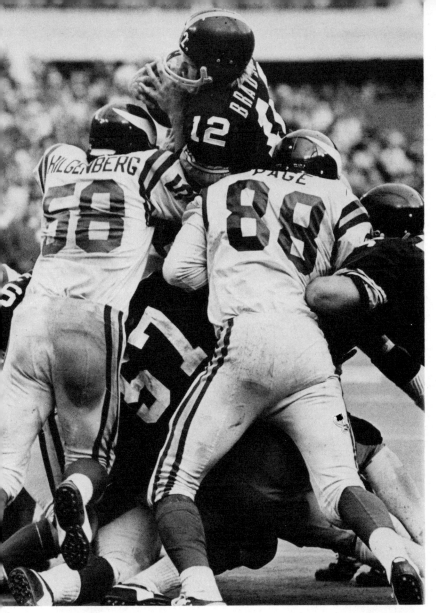

Pittsburgh quarterback Terry Bradshaw gets sacked by the Minnesota Vikings during his rookie year.

After about ten minutes, the coach walked over to Terry, put his arm around him, and asked, "How did I miss you, son?" He then told the youngster to pick up a uniform after practice.

Bradshaw never forgot the excitement of that moment. "I picked up my uniform and ran all the way home," he said years later. "I tore into the house jumping up and down, screaming and hollering, 'I made it! I made it! I've got a uniform and I'm on the football team!' I hugged everybody and ran around the house like a crazy man. I just couldn't believe it."

By the time he was a sophomore at Woodlawn High School, Bradshaw was a starting quarterback. Unfortunately, he was starting for the junior varsity because the varsity had an All-America star calling signals. It wasn't until his senior year that Bradshaw started for the varsity. And even then, he wasn't a real sensation. Although he had a good season, he didn't even make the All-City team in Shreveport, much less All-State or All-America. In fact, Terry was far more successful at track than at football.

The holder of the American schoolboy javelin record (244 feet 11 inches), Terry got over two hundred track scholarship offers from colleges all over the country. But he didn't even consider them. "As far as I was concerned, the javelin was trifling and unimportant compared to football," he explained.

Bradshaw got only three offers to play college football, and he chose Louisiana Tech. There was no freshman team at Tech, so Terry found himself on the varsity in a familiar role—benchwarmer. He got so discouraged that after a year he tried to transfer to Florida State. But during the off-season, Tech hired a new head coach, Maxie Lambright. As his first official act, Lambright told his players that everyone's position was now up for grabs.

Bradshaw wound up sharing the starting quarterback job as a sophomore and passed for 951 yards. By the following year the starting slot belonged to Bradshaw alone. Making up for lost time, Terry set over 20 school and conference records in his final two college seasons.

Bradshaw, also known as "The Blond Bomber" and "The Rifleman," became a legend in the Southeast. But nationally, Tech was a relatively little-known school. ("Louisiana what?" people joked.) So Bradshaw did not get the great publicity that was showered on stars from the major football powers. Nevertheless, NFL scouts were well aware of "The Rifleman," and they were awed by what they saw.

The Steelers would be picking first in the 1970 college draft, and they'd been interested in Bradshaw for quite a while. One day a scout showed up at Ruston, Louisiana, for a Tech game. He saw Bradshaw flick his wrist and line a spiral 55 yards downfield as he was being dragged down by five tacklers. "I might as well have seen a flying saucer," the scout said. "Nobody's gonna believe me when I tell them about this."

The rest of the country had its first opportunity to see Bradshaw early in 1970, when he was invited to play against the pros in the nationally televised Senior Bowl in Mobile, Alabama. Playing with a pulled hamstring muscle, Terry still had a super day. He completed 17 of

30 passes for 267 yards and two touchdowns, and he was named the game's Most Valuable Player. A thousand miles up north in cold, snowy Pittsburgh, he was named savior of the Steelers, who had just finished a dismal 1–13 season.

The St. Louis Cardinals offered the Steelers four starters for the rights to Bradshaw. The Philadelphia Eagles also offered four veterans. And the Atlanta Falcons practically offered their entire roster. "Take the ones you want," said Falcon general manager and head coach Norm Van Brocklin. "Take as many as you want."

Art Rooney, Sr., the Steelers' owner, refused all offers. "Our scouts told us that a quarterback prospect like this kid comes along only once every ten or twelve years," Rooney recalled. "I was tired of giving away great players and then suffering through fifteen years of them coming back to town with other teams, quarterbacks especially—Johnny Unitas, Lenny Dawson, Jack Kemp, Bill Nelsen, Earl Morrall. We even had the rights to Sid Luckman and lost those. I didn't want to see it happen again."

Pittsburgh fans were as excited as the Steeler management about Bradshaw. Fans, coaches, and sportswriters all expected an instant Steeler championship with Bradshaw the Bomber leading the charge.

Bradshaw's college coach, Maxie Lambright, sounded the only note of caution. "Terry is a strong, natural passer and an athlete with a lot of courage," said Lambright, "but he's facing a great transition.

"He's always been a very physical player, one who

never minded tucking the ball away and running. Well, he'll have to be more careful about that now. Some of those 260-pound linemen would love to tear into a quarterback rolling out there unprotected.

"Terry has a quick, accurate arm. He can really drill the ball to a receiver, even when he's throwing off balance. But he's going to have to learn not to turn the ball loose without recognizing what the defense is doing. In college football he may have seen three varieties of defense. In pro football he may see ten varieties of defense. There will be a much greater burden on him, and I hope everyone realizes he'll need some time to adjust to it."

But time to adjust and develop was a luxury denied to Bradshaw. The Steelers and their fans had waited a long time for a winner. They reasoned that if the kid was as good as everyone said he was, he should immediately start tearing the NFL apart.

And during the 1970 exhibition schedule, that's exactly what the big rookie did. In the first exhibition game, against the Miami Dolphins, he replaced starting quarterback Terry Hanratty in the second half. When Hanratty left the game the Steelers were trailing, 13–0. Bradshaw closed the gap to 16–10. And even though Pittsburgh lost the game, Bradshaw's fine performance won him the starting job.

That was the beginning of a brief but glorious success story for the rookie quarterback. During the next two weeks, he led Pittsburgh to victories over the Minnesota Vikings, the New York Giants, the Boston Patriots, and the Oakland Raiders. Steeler fans were ecstatic, and so

Bradshaw covers a bobbled hand-off during a 1971 exhibition game against the New York Giants.

was Bradshaw. "I was on cloud nine," he recalled. "Everything was great."

Terry's happiness didn't last long, however. Exhibition games are just what their name implies. They give coaches a chance to evaluate and teach. Teams stick to basics. Winning is nice, but not paramount. Of course, all that changes once the regular season begins. Then it counts. Then winning is everything. And once the regular season began, Terry and the Steelers began losing.

Bradshaw played badly in the opener, and the Steelers lost to Houston, 19–7. Terry completed only 4 of 16 passes and suffered the embarrassment of being tackled in the end zone for a safety. He cried in the shower after the game. He couldn't sleep that night. His dream of glory was turning into a nightmare.

The following week the Steelers lost to the Denver Broncos, and the week after that they bowed to the Cleveland Browns. In both games Bradshaw was dropped for safeties. The Browns sacked him a total of seven times. "I was learning fast that pro linemen were bigger and faster and tougher to elude than college linemen," Terry said.

Suddenly, super-rookie Bradshaw could do nothing right. His play-calling became uncertain. His passes were tentative and erratic. "I felt my confidence oozing away," he said. It was terrible, because I knew that was the one thing I needed most. Because I felt I was losing it, I started pressing. I pressed awfully hard to get the one big play, trying to get ahead."

No matter how hard he tried, though, Bradshaw just

couldn't please the fans. Sportswriters joined the critics, too. According to Terry, they characterized him as "a big, dumb, small-college, Southern, rural, bible-totin' kid. A hick, that's what they painted me as—a hick."

As the season progressed, things got worse for Bradshaw instead of better. He was forced to share playing time with Hanratty, which made his confidence plummet to an all-time low. And later Terry got into head coach Chuck Noll's doghouse when fog grounded his flight out of Shreveport and made him miss a valuable day of practice. A frustrated Bradshaw was benched against Cincinnati and watched Hanratty lead the Steelers to a 21–10 victory.

Standing next to Hanratty in the locker room after the game, Bradshaw popped off to sportswriters. "I don't want to play second fiddle to Hanratty," he said. "I don't mind playing behind somebody older, someone ready to retire, but I surely won't play behind someone my age. If the Steelers are going to do that, they'd better trade me."

It was a thoughtless comment, and it cost Bradshaw dearly. "I think Terry lost the respect of some guys when he made that crack about being traded, which was a rap at Hanratty," said a teammate at the time. "Heck, Hanratty didn't gripe when Noll played Bradshaw. He took it like a pro. As a veteran, Hanratty had more reason to gripe than a rookie did."

"I'll bet eighty percent of the guys would rather have Hanratty playing," added another Steeler.

And a grim-faced coach Noll snapped, "Terry has a lot of growing up to do—both on the field and off it."

Bradshaw finished out the season with little success. "By the time it ended, I just wanted to get away from Pittsburgh," he recalled. "All I wanted was to go home. I wanted away from sports, football particularly. I wanted to relax and get football out of my mind.

"But by February, I was mentally ready and anxious for the season to start. I knew I had to beat out Hanratty and that would be a battle from the beginning. I was just going to make doggone sure I was in the right frame of mind, even if that was hard for me because I had such a bad rookie year. Everybody else was doing his job. It was I who wasn't doing mine. I must have been something to look at—the comic-strip kid, the country bumpkin, the savior of the team. It was too much for a 21-year-old kid, too much for me."

Bradshaw managed to win the starting job from Hanratty in 1971, but his troubles weren't over yet. Although the Steelers steadily improved, winning their first division championship in 1972, then tying the Cincinnati Bengals for the division title in '73, it was no thanks to Bradshaw. In only one of the three seasons did Terry complete as many as half of his passes. And his interceptions outnumbered his touchdown tosses, 49–35. His play remained frustratingly inconsistent. And he continued to suffer embarrassing lapses like the time he forgot the snap count. Another time he was openly defied in the huddle after calling a running play on a third-and-25 situation from his own 13-yard line in the fourth quarter of a game in which the Steelers trailed by 14 points. "One of the guys grabbed him and insisted he change the call," recalled one Steeler.

Disappointed Steeler fans gave up on Bradshaw and, at times, turned on him viciously. In 1973 he suffered a shoulder injury during a game. As he knelt in pain, clutching his shoulder, the crowd at Pittsburgh's Three Rivers Stadium actually cheered. The injured quarterback sat out the rest of the year.

By the start of the 1974 season, Bradshaw had lost his starting job to a third-year man, Joe Gilliam, who had thrown only 71 regular-season passes as a pro. "I never really knew how much the job meant to me until I lost it," said Bradshaw.

Gilliam and Hanratty alternated at quarterback. But neither seemed able to move the team. By midseason Pittsburgh's offense was still faltering. In desperation, the Steelers decided to give Bradshaw another chance at quarterback.

Bradshaw made the most of that chance, and Pittsburgh started scoring more. Veteran Steeler Ray Mansfield was particularly impressed with Bradshaw's performance in a December victory over the New England Patriots. "He got clobbered three times in a row right at the beginning of the game," Mansfield recalled. "I thought he'd be afraid to throw a pass after that. But the very next time we got the ball he came out passing. In the huddle he didn't seem as confused as he used to be. He used to get confused in tough situations. Like when we had our back to the goal line or were hit with a penalty. He had more composure now. I guess you call it maturity. He came into that huddle and he was in complete charge."

Pittsburgh's victory over New England had clinched

Terry drops back to pass during a game against the Cincinnati Bengals.

another Steeler divisional crown. And two weeks later Bradshaw led his teammates to a big win over Buffalo in the opening round of the playoffs. "I've never seen Brad so in command," marveled offensive tackle John Kolb after the game. "He's calling the plays coolly and quickly."

"The bad days are behind me," Bradshaw happily told a crowd of reporters. "You guys keep asking me if I've 'arrived.' I don't know what you're talking about. Every day I work to improve myself. I'm better than I was yesterday, but probably not as good as I'll be tomorrow. I feel better than I've ever felt before—more mature, more confident. It's only natural that maturity would reflect in my performance."

The following week, the Steelers upset the heavily favored Oakland Raiders, 24–13, to win their long-awaited Super Bowl berth. And Bradshaw's ultimate vindication came two weeks later with Pittsburgh's 16–6 victory over the Minnesota Vikings in Super Bowl IX.

It had taken the Steelers 42 years to win their first league championship. But it took them only one year to win their second, thanks largely to Bradshaw's fine work in 1975. The Steelers went all the way to Super Bowl X, where they faced the Dallas Cowboys.

Pittsburgh took an early lead in that game, and with only three minutes remaining they were ahead 15–10. Then Bradshaw fired a 64-yard bomb to receiver Lynn Swann, who was standing in the clear on Dallas's 6-yard line. Swann streaked to the end zone with a touchdown, but Terry was blitzed just a split second after releasing the ball.

In Super Bowl X, Bradshaw gets off a pass despite the intimidating presence of Dallas's "Too Tall" Jones.

Bradshaw suffered a minor concussion on that play and had to go to the sidelines. But this time no one cheered about his injury except a few Dallas fans who hoped to see the Steelers fall apart without their leader. The Steelers hung on and defeated Dallas, 21–17, to win their second straight NFL title. And after the game, Terry Bradshaw was hailed as a genius by those same critics who had once called him a dummy.

O.J. SIMPSON

On a cold, snowy day in December 1973 the New York Jets played host to the Buffalo Bills at Shea Stadium. It was the final game of the regular season. The Jets were out of the running for the playoffs, and the Bills had only the slimmest hope of gaining a wildcard berth. Nevertheless, a nation of fans eagerly awaited the start of the game. The focus of their attention was Buffalo superstar O.J. Simpson, better known as "The Juice." This afternoon he would be trying to break one of pro football's most highly prized records—the single-season rushing mark of 1,863 yards set a decade earlier by Cleveland's legendary Jim Brown.

Simpson was having a great year so far. He needed just 61 more yards to break the record, and his Buffalo teammates were determined to help him get them. O.J. was far and away the most popular man on the team.

Now in the huddle, the Bills kept nudging him, urging, "Let's get it, Juice! Let's go! Let's go!"

The Juice went, all right—30 yards on Buffalo's second play from scrimmage. He kept on going, picking up 4 yards here, 7 yards there. Altogether, he gained 57 yards in less than ten minutes. Then he squirmed through a crack of daylight opened up by offensive tackle Donnie Green and guard Reggie McKenzie for another 6. That gave him a season's total of 1,869 yards.

Time was called as O.J. was surrounded by his happy teammates. The referee shook Simpson's hand and gave him the game ball. Even the Jet fans roared their approval for a great performance by a great competitor.

Play resumed, and O.J. continued piling up yardage. Early in the fourth quarter, Buffalo quarterback Joe Ferguson fired up the huddle by announcing, "O.K., guys, The Juice only needs sixty more yards."

Another 60 yards would give Simpson 2,000 for the season—a nice round number and a record that figured to last a long, long time. O.J. kept running, and with 5:56 to play, he was just four yards short of the magic number. Suddenly gloomy Shea was bathed in a million candlepowers' worth of light.

Ferguson called the signals. The ball was snapped, and he planted it right in Simpson's arms. The play was number 5 in the Buffalo repertoire—a straight off-tackle drive by O.J. behind the blocking of 243-pound fullback Jim Braxton.

Wide receiver J.D. Hill picked up a blitzing Jet linebacker and drove him to the outside. Left tackle

Dave Foley threw his 260-pound bulk into the Jet lineman opposite him and blasted him to the inside. Braxton rumbled straight ahead through the hole, knocking a Jet safety backwards. O.J. trotted behind Braxton, picking up an easy 7 yards. That run gave him 200 yards for the game and an amazing 2,003 for the season.

The Bills won the game, 34–14. But the big winner, of course, was O.J. Simpson. A special interview room had been set up to accommodate the overflow of writers and broadcasters that had gathered in anticipation of Simpson's big day. But when O.J. entered the room, he was not alone. To the amazement of the normally hard-bitten reporters, O.J. brought Braxton, Ferguson, and his entire offensive with him. After introducing his teammates, he gave a brief, highly complimentary biography of each and told how each had contributed to his record. "This line is good and it's young and it helped put me where I am now," O.J. said in conclusion. "I just wanted all of you to meet them."

Reggie McKenzie expressed the mutual feelings of the Bills. "O.J. is a warm-hearted, sincere guy, and there was no way the Jets were going to stop him," said the great Buffalo blocker. "We made sure of that. I mean, who else do you know who'd take the entire line to a national press conference? It was beautiful. He really meant it. He believes in himself, and he believes in us. . . . Man, blocking for The Juice! You just love to take that step and boom, bury your man!"

Later O.J. bought two dozen 14-karat gold bracelets for his teammates. Each was inscribed with two numbers—2,003 and 3,088 (the team's 1973 record rushing total)—and signed "The Juice." Said one recipient, "I had mine appraised at $1,000. It must have cost him $25,000 for all of them."

Simpson's generosity also took less tangible forms. He was never too busy to sign autographs or give a friendly hello to his fans. One day O.J. was relaxing in the locker room after a victory over the Falcons in Atlanta. He asked for a cold orange drink from a nearby cooler, and a young boy immediately stepped forward with a can.

"This one's warm," said O.J. "Will one of you guys throw me a cold one?"

The boy's father, one of the locker room attendants, whispered to O.J., "He's been waiting for an hour to give that to you."

"In that case," said O.J., turning to the boy and picking up the warm drink, "I'll not only drink it, I'll drink a toast to you, my friend."

The look on the boy's face was impossible to describe. But O.J. knew just how he felt. Simpson hadn't forgotten his first meeting with a real live superstar. It happened in San Francisco when O.J. was a boy. He and some friends had sneaked into Kezar Stadium to watch the Cleveland Browns play the San Francisco 49ers. Afterwards, they went to an ice cream parlor across the street from the ball park for a snack.

"We were just messin' around in there when who should walk in but Mr. Jim Brown himself," recalled Simpson. "Well, you know how kids are. We were awed, but we started fooling around, strutting, showing off,

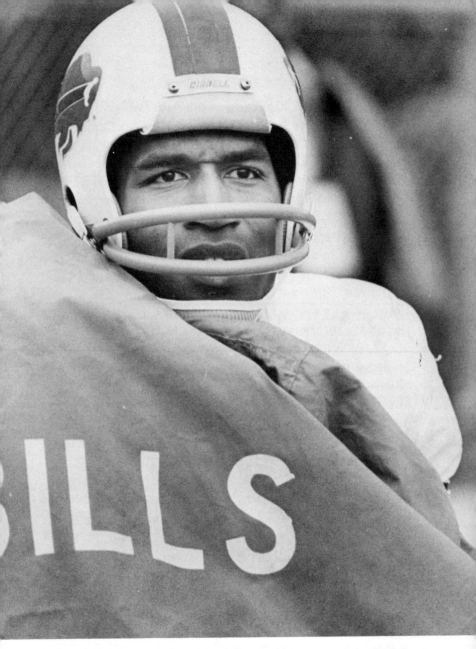

O.J. Simpson, Buffalo's all-star running back, set a new standard for rushing—2,003 yards gained in a single season.

mumbling things, and mimicking him behind his back. Finally I just walked right up to him and said, 'Jim Brown, you ain't so great. When I get to pro ball, I'm gonna break all your records.' I know it sounds unbelievable now, but I was just kidding around."

Brown had looked at the brash youngster, smiled, and said, "Well, you talk big now, but let's see what you do when you get the chance."

O.J. almost didn't get the chance. A product of a broken home, he grew up in a rough black ghetto in San Francisco. Simpson flirted with serious trouble several times as a youngster, the kind of trouble that leads to jail and a future without hope.

O.J.'s troubles began at birth when an aunt convinced his parents to name him Orenthal James. "She was always thinking up names like that for people in the family," said O.J. "She stuck another nephew with the name Gursel. It wouldn't have been so bad, except when she finally had kids of her own she named them Stuart and James."

O.J.'s nicknames were no improvement over his given name. He had very spindly legs because of a calcium deficiency he'd suffered as a baby, so the kids called him "Pencil Legs." They also called him "Headquarters" because his head looked too large for his thin body.

In grade school, O.J. became the leader of a street gang called the Superiors. The leader of a gang is usually its most accomplished troublemaker, and O.J. was a superstar there, too. He fought, he ran, he threw rocks, he cut school. He just avoided being arrested for car theft by outracing a pursuing policeman.

O.J. continued running wild at Galileo High School and was nearly suspended several times. Once he and some other boys were caught shooting dice in the boys' room. When the group was taken to the dean's office, O.J. lagged behind. He managed to convince the dean that he was just an innocent bystander.

O.J. never went to class if he could avoid it. The only reason he stayed in school at all was to play on the football team. With the exception of Simpson, however, it really wasn't much of a team. In O.J.'s junior year, Galileo lost 16 games in a row. The next year the team lost its first three games. The frustrated coach threatened to bench all his seniors if they didn't win their next game. O.J. made sure that they won. He scored three touchdowns to lead Galileo to a startling upset over a strong team from St. Ignatius. Had Galileo lost, O.J.'s career would have been over, and he almost certainly would have quit school.

Simpson made the All-City team as a senior at Galileo. His schoolwork was so poor, however, that he got only one half-hearted college offer. He considered joining the Army but finally decided to attend a two-year junior college, City College of San Francisco.

O.J. tore it up in junior college. As a freshman he gained 1,161 yards, averaging almost 10 yards per carry and scoring 26 touchdowns (a national junior college record). Scouts from four-year colleges flocked to see him, and scholarship offers poured in. O.J. wanted to go to the University of Southern California, and USC wanted him. But USC also wanted him to improve his grades by attending junior college for one more year.

O.J. agreed and used that extra year to good advantage. He racked up 1,391 yards and broke his own touchdown record with 28. More important, he developed the kind of work habits and mature outlook that would enable him to survive academically at USC.

When he finally entered USC, O.J. was a junior. The coaches wanted to see if the junior college hotshot was tough enough to play the all-important tailback position. In O.J.'s first practice session, head coach John McKay started him off with seven straight carries. Simpson got the job done, and made a believer out of McKay.

In his first year at USC, O.J. led the nation in rushing, made every All-America team, and finished second in the Heisman Trophy voting. In the last game of the season he sprinted 64 yards for the touchdown that gave USC a 21–20 victory over arch-rival UCLA. That win clinched the national championship for the USC Trojans. The Trojans were invited to the Rose Bowl, where they defeated Indiana 14–3. Simpson scored both USC touchdowns and was named the game's outstanding player.

When the football season ended, O.J. went out for track. A fine sprinter, he helped the USC 440-yard relay team set a world record.

O.J.'s senior year was equally outstanding. Although the season ended in a disappointing Rose Bowl defeat for the Trojans, O.J. racked up one success after another. During the regular season he set an NCAA rushing record with 1,709 yards. In his two years at USC, he'd equaled or broken 13 school records and led

Playing for the University of Southern California, O.J. (32) picks up some yardage against Indiana in the 1968 Rose Bowl.

the Trojans to a 19–2–1 record. Not surprisingly, he was awarded the Heisman Trophy as the nation's outstanding college player.

The Buffalo Bills made O.J. their number one pick in the 1969 college draft. After a lifetime spent in the warmth and sunshine of Southern California, O.J. wasn't very happy about playing in cold, snowy Buffalo. But after prolonged negotiations, he signed a four-year contract worth more than $300,000.

O.J. was even more unhappy when he got to Buffalo. The once-mighty Bills had fallen on hard times. Under coach Lou Saban, they had won the championship of the old American Football League in 1964 and '65. But when Saban left the Bills after the 1965 season, they fell apart. By 1968 they had deteriorated to a 1–12–1 record. The only good thing about that terrible season was the fact that it gave the Bills first choice in the '69 draft—namely, O.J. Simpson.

The Buffalo fans had resented Simpson's publicly stated lack of enthusiasm for their city. But he quickly won them over. He also got along well with his new teammates. Unfortunately, his relationship with head coach John Rauch was not as pleasant.

The problem was that O.J. was ready, willing, and able to carry the ball 30 or 40 times per game, just as he'd done at USC. But Rauch had other ideas. The Bills were used to playing a passing game. And Rauch saw no reason to change their style—even though they now had one of the greatest running backs to come along in years. "I couldn't build my offense around one back no matter how good he is," the coach said. "It's too easy for the pros to set up defensive keys."

The Bills' veteran quarterback, Jack Kemp, a fine passer, was delighted with Rauch's stand. O.J. was miserable. In his first three pro seasons, O.J. rushed 484 times for a total of just 1,327 yards. (In a single year at USC he'd done a lot better than that.)

As a rookie, the highly touted Simpson was a flop. By most standards his first-year statistics (677 yards rushing, 393 yards catching passes, and 559 yards running back kickoffs) would have been considered good. But Simpson wasn't supposed to be good—he was supposed to be great. His second season (1970) was another disappointment. Sidelined by a knee injury, he missed almost half the games.

Things got even worse in 1971. Rauch resigned and was replaced by Harvey Johnson, the team's fun-loving head scout. Johnson got along well with his players, but he wasn't a very effective coach. That season the Bills lost 13 of their 14 games.

It was a disastrous season for Simpson, too. In one game, a 43–0 loss to Baltimore, he rushed for *minus* ten yards. O.J. still wasn't getting the ball as often as he wished. And when he did get it, he couldn't do much because of the Bills' poor blocking. O.J. made no secret of his disgust with the situation and expressed a strong desire to leave Buffalo. "I'd just had three years of nothin'," he explained, "and I knew that while they might have some trouble trading me, there were teams that were interested."

Before the 1972 season got under way, however, O.J. changed his tune. The Bills announced that Lou Saban was returning as Buffalo head coach. His first message to O.J. gave new hope to the frustrated running back. It said: "Report to camp in shape because we're going to give you the football." Saban also promised to build a strong offensive line to give O.J. the kind of running room he needed.

That was just what O.J. had been waiting to hear. Now he made a vow to himself: No more dreaming of escape; he would sink or swim with the Bills. "I realized that it was time to stop thinking about playing out my option, getting traded, running away from the situation," he said. "I decided that whatever I might have thought as a kid, I had to accept the Bills as my team. We had cried together enough. I wanted to help us laugh together in the future."

The 1972 season produced some smiles. Although the Bills finished with a losing 4–9–1 record, it was their best effort in years. And O.J. had his best pro season yet. Behind a young patchwork offensive line, he led the NFL in rushing with 1,251 yards. And he carried the ball 292 times, 109 more carries than his '71 total. Simpson was thrilled with his progress and quick to share the credit with coach Saban. "Lou was my first real coach in the pros," O.J. said. "He turned us around and he saved my career."

Saban had big plans for the next season. In the 1973 college draft, he fulfilled his promise to O.J. by selecting two great college blockers—tight end Paul Seymour and guard Joe DeLamielleure. They joined Reggie McKenzie, who had enjoyed an outstanding rookie season at guard the year before; Dave Foley, a one-time pass-blocking Jet tackle who had been claimed on waivers by Buffalo in 1972; and two third-year pros just coming into their own, tackle Donnie Green and center Bruce Jarvis. Injured at mid-season, Jarvis was ably replaced by Mike Montler, a fifth-year man obtained in a trade with New England.

O.J. started off the '73 season with high hopes. During training camp he shared his feelings with Reggie McKenzie. "You know, with the guys we've got to block, I think I should gain 1,700 yards this year," Simpson predicted. "Maybe I'll even have a shot at Jim Brown's record."

McKenzie was even more ambitious. "Why don't we go for the two grand?" he asked.

A 2,000-yard season seemed an impossible dream at the time. But O.J. began to make it a reality from the opening game. That day Simpson gained 250 yards against the New England Patriots to set an NFL single-game rushing record. When asked his opinion of the Bills' superstar, rookie Patriot defensive end Ray Hamilton admitted only half-jokingly, "I never got close enough to find out."

That was fine with O.J. He saw no point in physically challenging tacklers. He preferred to rely on his slick moves, rocket acceleration, and uncanny peripheral vision to avoid them. "I don't go looking to stick my head in where it can get broken," O.J. explained. "I remember the first time I faced Dick Butkus when he was really the main bad dude of the league. Some guys said you have to challenge Butkus and show him you can hit with him. I said, 'Oh no, I want to show him that

47

With a good block from teammate Reggie McKenzie, O.J. makes a record-breaking run against the New York Jets in 1973.

I'm so quick he can't hit me.' "

Behind the Bills' fine blocking, O.J. was rarely hit in the games that followed. And he kept gaining more and more yardage. Early in the season, Reggie McKenzie nicknamed the Buffalo's offensive line "The Electric Company" because "it turns The Juice on."

O.J. wound up the season with more than his record "two grand." He also set new NFL standards for most carries in a season (332) and in a single game (39), most 100-yard games in a season (11), and most 200-yard games (3). And the Bills finished with a winning 9–5 record.

O.J. was quite a star during the off-season, too. He received numerous offers for speaking engagements, commercial endorsements, and motion picture roles. He accepted parts in two movies: *The Klansman*, with Lee Marvin and Richard Burton, and *The Towering Inferno*, with Steve McQueen and Paul Newman.

When the 1974 season began, however, O.J. devoted all his energy to football. But although the Electric Company continued its fine blocking, O.J. found it harder than ever to elude opposing defenders. After his record-shattering '73 season, they were always looking for him. Fortunately, the development of the Bills' second-year quarterback Joe Ferguson enabled Buffalo to pass more and take the defensive heat off Simpson. Handicapped all year by a sore knee, O.J. rushed only 270 times, and his yardage total dropped to 1,125, third best in the league. Nevertheless, the Bills again finished with a 9–5 record, and they made the playoffs for the first time since 1966.

Simpson gallops through the Green Bay defense in a 1975 game.

By then O.J. had won just about every individual honor a player can win. But he still had one more ambition—to play on a championship team. Once the Bills achieved that, Simpson felt he could leave football without regrets to pursue his many outside activities.

O.J. was as good as ever on the football field in 1975. He led the league with 1,817 yards rushing, the third greatest total in history. His 23 touchdowns broke former Chicago Bear star Gale Sayers's NFL record by one.

A highlight of the season came in a game against the Pittsburgh Steelers, the defending Super Bowl champs. O.J. took off on an incredible 88-yard scoring dash that left the Steelers shaking their heads in admiration. "All I saw," moaned all-pro linebacker Jack Ham, "was the back of his jersey—for 80 yards." And Steeler coach Chuck Noll added, "An ordinary runner we would've had for a loss. Only one man could have done that to us."

Mean Joe Greene, Pittsburgh's huge tackle, was so frustrated he decided to take the law into his own hands. Later in the game, Buffalo center Mike Montler prepared for the snap—only to find Greene's large foot planted firmly on the football. "I'm not gonna let you snap this thing," roared Greene, the NFL's most ferocious lineman. "O.J.'s been going by me all day. You start this play and I'll break you in half."

At the end of the season, O.J. began talking about leaving the game. "I was reading an article not long ago that said a man reaches his absolute peak, mentally and physically, at 26," O.J. explained. "Alexander the Great had his best season at 26. Beethoven wrote his best symphony at 26. I ran for 2,003 yards at 26. I'm sure guys do fine things before and after, but after that age, whether you know it or not, it's downhill.

"I can't go on much longer," Simpson continued. "I'm 28 now and I look around at the other backs who came in with me and they're all limping around. I realize what can happen. I really don't know anything definite about the future. The thing is, I'm looking for the right opportunity in movies that will give me longevity and security. I haven't decided whether I'm going to play next year or not. After the season, I'll sit down and talk it over with my wife and my agent."

Happily for all pro football fans, Simpson decided to continue to play. If as he claimed, O.J. was leveling off, no one else was aware of it. To anyone interested in the game—fans, coaches, and players alike—he remained The Juice, the finest runner of his era and perhaps the finest ever.

BILL BERGEY

Every fall and winter, during the four to five months of
the National Football League season, Micky Bergey
gets the feeling that she's married to two men—Dr.
Jekyll and Mr. Hyde! From Sunday night to Thursday,
her husband, Bill Bergey, is a soft-spoken family man,
who behaves like the banker he is in the off-season. But
from Thursday to Sunday night, the middle linebacker
of the Philadelphia Eagles, becomes a completely different person . . . or creature. Dark, coarse hair suddenly grows out of his face and body. His fingernails
become claws; his teeth, fangs. He bays at the moon,
eats raw meat, and must be chained to the wall at night.
At least that's what the people who play against him
claim.

"I find myself starting to get keyed up on Thursday
for a Sunday game," Bergey explained. "I direct every-

thing I do at 1 P.M. Sunday, when I have to reach my exploding point. I reach an emotional pitch, and after the game I'm all nerves and frazzled ends. It's funny, but after a game, no matter how physical it is, I'm never tired. I can't sleep. So I sit up all night with my little son, Jason. We play in the living room with his toys and tanks and trucks and stuff, and then about 6 A.M. I go out to a truck stop for bacon and eggs. Then when I get home, I can sleep. And it starts all over again the next Thursday."

To excel in professional football, particularly on defense, requires a great commitment to the game. All players must maintain a certain cool to carry out their assignments, but once they get beyond that, football becomes largely a brutal test of who runs faster, hits harder, and lasts longer. Since most football pros are incredibly fit physically, it's the player with the best emotional edge who often comes out on top. It was the emotional demands of his job that made 6-foot-2, 253-pound Bill Bergey a monster for half the week during the season. But it was Bill's physical response to those demands that made him one of the very best linebackers in the game.

In his early years, however, it seemed unlikely that Bergey would make it to college, much less to the pros. Bill was a great high school football player in his hometown of South Dayton, New York. But he was such a poor student that college scouts stayed away. He attracted lukewarm attention from only one college—small, obscure Arkansas State. And even there he had to sell himself to the coach, Benny Ellender.

Ellender was attending a coach's clinic near South Dayton when he was visited by Bergey and a host of Bill's fans (mostly relatives). Bergey didn't have game films of himself to show, but he delivered an earnest sales pitch, accompanied by a scrapbook full of his exploits as, of all things, a pole vaulter. "I was a 205-pound pole vaulter who broke a school record once at 11 feet 3 inches," Bergey said. "Now that's getting a lot of load off the ground."

Impressed with Bergey's agility, strength, and obvious desire, Ellender offered him a partial scholarship. "I think it was only something like $160 a semester," Bergey recalled, "but it seemed like a million." "And my grades improved so much there you wouldn't believe it. I even made the dean's list a couple of times."

Arkansas State got a million-dollar athlete for its small investment. "He came to us as a 205-pound fullback," said Bill Davidson, an assistant who went on to become the school's head coach. "Bill could stand flatfooted and do a full back somersault with a half-twist and land back on his feet. He could do a two-and-a-half off a three-meter diving board. That's how agile the guy was.

"We couldn't keep him off the trampoline. He was always big on tumbling and could do all sorts of flips that made the gymnastic team members green with envy."

Bergey was also doing all sorts of flips on the football field, moving from running back to defensive middle guard then back to offense at a guard spot. Finally, he was switched to middle linebacker in the spring of 1966 and suddenly everything clicked, including a full scholarship.

"He was a real razzle-dazzle player, a crowd pleaser," recalled Gerald Jumper, who played split end on the same team. "You always knew the Monk [Bill's college nickname] was around. He was a man in motion all the time, and he always liked to hit real hard. Nothing pleased him more than to grab a player, wrestle with him, throw him down to the ground, and then just stand there and glare at him."

"He was not a dirty player by design," said Andy Morris, sports information director back then. "Sometimes he just let his emotions run a little wild. But the intensity of his positive attitude obviously rubbed off on the other players."

As a senior, Bergey was credited with an incredible 25 tackles per game, and was named a little All-America. He was also chosen the Most Valuable Player of the post-season North-South Shrine game and the Pecan Bowl.

The Cincinnati Bengals made Bergey their second-round pick in the 1969 college draft. And when they saw him in action against the Super Bowl champion New York Jets in the College All-Star game they knew they had picked a winner. General manager and head coach Paul Brown was particularly impressed by his rookie's effort in a goal-line stand that stopped the Jets from scoring after they had gotten a first down on the All-Stars' 3-yard line.

Playing in the College All-Star game was a big honor for Bergey, but it was a mixed blessing. It delayed the start of his training-camp education for a critical few weeks. A rookie's first training camp is a demanding, bewildering, frustrating, often frightening experience under the best of circumstances. But Bergey was operating under the additional handicap of trying to master one of the game's most difficult positions.

"I can't get over the transition from college to pro football," Bergey admitted midway through the camp. "I thought it would be competitive, and it is. But I didn't think I'd have to learn every pass pattern and pass play of the offense. But that's what they want. The coach wants us to be able to come in and put each play on the blackboard every day after practice.

"I just can't sleep at night. I lie awake thinking of those plays, all the responsibilities I have. I'd just love to lie down and shut my eyes and go to sleep."

Despite the difficulties, Bergey was delighted to be with the Bengals. "I wouldn't trade this life for anything," he said. "If a person doesn't love this game, there's no sense being here."

The Bengals were equally happy with Bergey. "He makes mistakes," linebacker coach Vince Costello said, "but he has the uncoachable ability to recover from most of them in a hurry, often without serious damage. There aren't many like that."

Bergey also had the kind of aggressiveness that can't be taught. You either have it or you don't—and Bergey definitely had it. In one exhibition game, he rattled the bones of Denver Bronco running back Tom Smiley, an old college foe, and exclaimed, "I really wanted a chunk of him."

Bergey got married in October of his rookie year, and Micky Bergey immediately found out what being a pro football wife is all about. For their honeymoon, Bill took her to the movies. The flick, playing in their own living room, was of an actual game between the Buffalo Bills and the then Boston Patriots. "I wanted to show her the center I'd be playing against in Buffalo in our next game," explained Bill.

Bill's studying paid off. He immediately became a Bengal starter. And at the end of the season, he was named the AFL's Defensive Rookie of the Year.

Bergey kept up the good work in 1970. That year he was named to the league's All-Star team and was voted his team's Most Valuable Player. Already Bergey had a reputation as one of the league's toughest defensemen. But it wasn't until the following season that the Pittsburgh Steelers found out just how tough he was. In a 1971 game a Bergey tackle sent Steeler quarterback Terry Bradshaw to the hospital for observation. Then Bergey blitzed Terry Hanratty, Bradshaw's replacement, and sent him to the sidelines with injured ribs.

Bergey continued to tear up the league for the next few years, and he was the undisputed leader of the Bengals' defense. But then in 1974 he made the startling announcement that he would be jumping to the new World Football League in 1976 when his Bengal contract expired. The WFL Washington Capitols had offered him a three-year deal for $525,000, and Bergey accepted.

The Cincinnati fans were shocked, then angry. Hate mail poured in. "I was being condemned because I was

**Playing for the Cincinnati Bengals in 1972, middle linebacker Bill Bergey
tackles Pittsburgh's Preston Pearson.**

In a 1973 game against the Denver Broncos, Bergey gets running back Floyd Little by the jersey.

trying to improve myself financially, to secure my family's future," said Bergey. "I was making $39,000 a year and had a chance to quadruple that. Is that so terrible?"

The Bengals seemed to think it was. They filed suit against Bergey and the WFL, charging that Bergey could not perform for one club while being paid bonus money by another and still be loyal.

"I said that was untrue and foolish," said Bergey, shaking his head in disgust. "A player should have enough personal desire to excel in each game, especially if he plays a position like middle linebacker. Did they really think I would sit back and take it easy out there? Listen, I don't enjoy getting hurt that much."

The Bengals also wanted to prevent Bergey from promoting the WFL while he was still playing in the NFL. But U.S. District Court Judge David S. Porter ruled against the Bengals. He declared that the WFL was within its rights to compete in an open market for players under NFL contract.

"I was glad to see it all end because it was a physical drain on my family," said Bergey. "But I must admit it was like a big football game to me. And I had won the game."

After the case was settled, however, Bergey had second thoughts about joining the WFL. The Washington Capitols moved to Virginia and then to Florida. Bergey found himself questioning the new league's stability and decided to stay in the established NFL. (It turned out to be a wise decision—the WFL went out of business after just two seasons.)

About that time, Bart Brown, Bergey's attorney, began getting phone calls from Eagles' owner Leonard Tose. Lots of them. Ironically, one of the witnesses who had testified against Bergey in court was Eagle coach Mike McCormack. "I remember saying to myself, 'I wouldn't want to play on your raunchy team anyway. I'd rather be traded to Saskatchewan for a snowmobile,' " Bergey recalled with a smile.

"Bart kept telling me to at least give the Philadelphia people a chance to talk," Bergey continued. "I could still see McCormack's face in that courtroom. But since I didn't want to be juggled around the NFL for the next few years, I consented.

"The conference lasted about three hours. Mike gave his theory about football and Leonard explained how he had set up the Eagles' organization. After they told me all about the Eagles, I figured that if the information was only one-tenth correct, I'd like to go there. That's how much they sold me on the club. So I turned to Bart and said, 'I don't know how you can do it, but get me to Philadelphia if you can.' "

The Bengals agreed to let the Eagles have Bergey. In return, Philadelphia traded away its number one draft pick in 1977, and its first two picks in 1978. Bergey signed a five-year, $500,000 contract with the Eagles on July 10, 1974.

At first, the Eagles and their fans thought the club's front office had made a bad deal by giving up a large chunk of its future for one player. In his first performance as an Eagle (in an exhibition against the Atlanta Falcons) Bergey did little to change their minds. In fact,

Playing for the Philadelphia Eagles in 1974, Bergey runs into two Giant blockers—and Doug Kotar (44) runs to the end zone.

he played one of his worst games ever. "It was a pressure thing for me," Bergey admitted. "I wanted to make a lot of plays when I first came here, sort of to prove myself to the coaches and teammates."

Bill was no more impressive in his second appearance—another exhibition, this time in Cincinnati against his former teammates. The Bengal fans showed they neither forgot nor forgave, by loudly jeering and cursing him.

Bergey was his own worst critic, however. "The first game against Atlanta—I couldn't believe it was me playing, I was so horrible," he said. "And the following week in Cincinnati, I wanted to perform well so I could feel good about that later on. But I played poorly there. As a matter of fact, I never made a tackle until the third quarter."

As soon as the regular season got under way, however, Bergey stopped pressing and became the defensive leader the Eagles were looking for. Philadelphia had tried no fewer than nine players at middle linebacker in the last three seasons, and none had taken hold. But now with Bergey in the line-up, the Eagles were finally satisfied.

"Bill Bergey is as good a linebacker as I've seen," said Walt Michaels, Philadelphia's defensive coordinator. "Bill knows how to gather himself. Some boxers are always on their toes and never in balance to deliver a blow. Same way with some pitchers, or quarterbacks, who throw only with the arm. Well, Bergey delivers with his body. You don't coach that and you can't teach that. That's instinct."

Coach McCormack, Bergey's one-time foe, was equally enthusiastic about the Eagles' new linebacker. "Bill has worked hard to develop what he calls his shoulder punch," said McCormack. "He just explodes those last six inches when he tackles a man."

Bergey's lethal shoulder punch was just one of the assets he brought to the Eagles. Less tangible but equally valuable was his strong leadership. Bergey was eager to share his love of the game with his new teammates. He wanted the Eagle defense to be a close unit, not just a collection of individuals. "Before every defensive series, we put our hands together in the center," Bergey said. "We have to keep that oneness. They try to put all this togetherness on me and that's not so. Everybody out there contributes."

Bergey's aggressiveness was contagious. His teammates began to copy his bruising style of play, and the Eagle defense became known as "Bergey's Brawlers." Some critics claimed that Bill's love of contact occasionally crossed that hard-to-define line separating legitimate aggressiveness and dirty play.

Bergey had obviously given some thought to that charge. After all, he'd been hearing it in one form or another for most of his career. "When I was playing high school football the hometown people said I'd never make it, that I was too reckless," he said heatedly, his bushy eyebrows moving up and down. "I tried to tell them that hard, aggressive football was my style. Blood and guts—their blood, my guts.

"Then when I finally made it to the pros, I was condemned for being a dirty cheap-shot artist. For crying out loud, if someone was trying to rip off *my* head, I'd call him that, too! Do I think I'm extra rough? No, I don't think so. Well, I really don't know. Maybe in the heat of battle I am . . . a little bit . . . I don't know. Look at it this way. Football's been real good to me, it's everything. So if we ever go all the way, if I can try extra hard for a game that's done so much for me, it will be a very rewarding thing for me."

Micky Bergey was even more vehement in her response to the criticism of her husband. "The image of Bill is so misleading," she said. "He's like two different people sometimes. He's competitive and hard-driving, but he's also very sensitive and emotional. When our first child, Jason, was born, he just burst into tears. At first I thought something was wrong with the baby. Then I realized he was just being emotional. It said a lot to me."

But whether he was too tough or just tough enough, Bergey was quick to point out that there's more to being a good defenseman than pure brute strength. "It's the mental part of this game that's an enormous challenge, especially for a middle linebacker," he explained. "I'm the quarterback of the defense, and what I do coordinates the line with the outside linebackers, and the outside linebackers with the backs. There's a lot of study and a lot of responsibility, and I strongly feel the middle linebacker must lead the team in tackles, because he has the option, in most cases, of getting to where the play is. . . .

"Basically, it comes down to covering the run and the pass equally well. I can't let a guy get past me carrying

Bergey hangs on to the ball after making an interception in a 1975 game against the San Francisco 49ers.

the ball, and if any receiver gets into my area, I've got to make sure he doesn't catch the ball. . . .

"In my first year, I played the pass poorly. In my second year, it was the same. So in my third year I worked hard on the pass and I lost my feel for the run. Then three years ago, it came together and it stayed that way. It really takes about four or five years until everything sinks in. It's got to be instinctive, you know. You can't waste much time thinking."

Bill Bergey didn't waste much time talking, either. And in his case, actions definitely spoke louder than words.

KEN HOUSTON

"Back in 1970 I dreamed I had intercepted a pass and was coming back with a beautiful return," said strong safety Ken Houston. "There was only one bad thing about it. Just as I crossed into the end zone, the official dropped a flag and I lost the touchdown on a clipping penalty."

The dream was so vivid that the next day Houston went over it with a local radio announcer, step by step. "Afterwards, I was glad I did," he said. "Nobody would have believed me. "That afternoon I intercepted a ball exactly where the dream had it, and I took the same route all the way to the goal line. In fact, just as I went in, I turned around to see the clip."

Happily for Houston, the dream fizzled right there. No clip. Touchdown! Ken's ability to intercept passes gave nightmares to the league's best quarterbacks and receivers. In his great pro career, first with the Houston Oilers and later with the Washington Redskins, Ken was a constant threat on defense. Time after time, he'd grab a rival's pass and run it all the way back for the score.

Ken was a standout from the time he joined the Oilers as a rookie in 1967. But his most amazing performance came in 1971. In the Oilers' last game of that season, against the San Diego Chargers, he intercepted two passes and returned one of them 38 yards and the other 29 yards for touchdowns. That gave him an NFL career record of nine touchdowns on interceptions, a single-season mark of four, and tied him for most in a game.

The only thing that surprised Ken about setting such a spectacular career record in just five seasons of play is that it took him so long. "I had seven touchdowns before I realized there was anything special about it," he said. "I thought the record must be about twenty, at least. When they told me it was seven and I was one shy of breaking it, I decided to go out and get it. I feel I could have broken it years ago. I dropped a few that would have been easy touchdowns my first year or two. I just wasn't concentrating."

There is nothing in football quite so demoralizing to players on a team as having one of their passes picked off and run back for a score. "They have the ball, and they think they're going in," Houston explained. "But all of a sudden I have it, and I'm going in. It kills them. It can be a fourteen-point play. They lose seven—we make seven."

First, of course, the defenseman must catch the ball before he can run with it. But that's not as easy as it sounds. According to Ken, most defensive backs drop more than they catch. "I used to," he admitted. "But it's just a bad habit. All you have to do is concentrate and practice catching. You seldom get a good ball, you know. They don't lay the pass up for you like they do for their own receivers. You're almost always twisted around in some awkward position, and here comes the ball. You've got to practice holding it standing on your head."

Catching the ball is just the beginning, though. "You have to plan the return," Ken said. "You have to think touchdown all the way. I want to get my interceptions on the sideline and head for the middle of the field. That gets the flow started. And when it's nicely under way, when everybody on both teams is sprinting for the center of the field, that's the time to cut back. If you're lucky, you go in."

The fact that he's facing offensive rather than defensive specialists helps a man returning an interception. "Offensive guys are not poor tacklers, exactly," Houston said. "They just don't practice tackling. They practice blocking—which is different. Offensive players also have a wait-and-see thing when they go on defense. They tend to wait and see if the other guy makes the tackle."

Against San Diego during that record-setting afternoon back in 1971, it was a matter of now you see Houston, now you don't for the frustrated Charger offense. "I wanted the record that day," Ken said, "and I went after it in that game.

75

"The touchdowns came back to back on successive plays in less than a minute. On one of them, Mike Garrett had a chance to cut me off. But he tried to block me. He wanted to roll me out of bounds, but he threw the block too low. I was lucky there. Garrett is a fine blocker."

Ken was delighted with his record, but he didn't expect it to last long. "I can see fifteen being the record," he said. "Guys like Lem Barney, Bill Bradley, and Lemar Parrish at Cincinnati—they score quite a bit. I'd like to keep the record for awhile. If I got fifteen, it would be safe five or six years. So I'm sure going to try for fifteen—next season."

Ken Houston didn't start playing strong safety until he turned pro, a common occurrence among NFL defensive backs. Ken was born and raised in Lufkin, Texas, a small town of approximately 22,000 residents. He played center and defensive tackle in high school. And at Prairie View (Texas) College he played center and middle linebacker.

"When I started playing football, it was more or less an escape for me," Houston recalled. "We were not a poor family, but we didn't have as much as some others. I was jealous of the things other guys had, so I used to take it out on them on the football field. There it was all basic. I had the same shoes they did, the same uniform, and I excelled."

Houston suffered back and knee injuries at college, so he didn't think much about a pro career. But the Houston Oilers did some serious thinking about him. They thought he had a wealth of raw ability and pro

Playing for the Oilers in 1969, strong safety Ken Houston (29) pulls down a pass intended for Jet receiver Don Maynard.

potential—but not as a linebacker. "He was only 190 pounds," recalled Oiler scout Tom Williams, "but he was one of the hardest-hitting tacklers for his size that I've seen. I knew he wasn't big enough to be a linebacker in the pros, but I figured with his speed and height he had a good chance to make it as a safety-man."

The Oilers had just finished the 1966 season with a dismal 3–11 record, so they needed all the help they could get. Williams invited Houston (the player) to Houston (the city) for a tryout. The Oilers were impressed enough to sign Ken for a modest bonus of approximately $5,000.

Although Ken had never played free safety before, he was willing to give it a try. But his first attempt at the Oilers' training camp was a total disaster. "I found myself with the habit of running back five or six yards and stopping, just as I had done as a middle line-backer," he laughingly recalled years later.

Ken felt more like crying at the time, however. It was embarrassing when the receiver kept right on going downfield, unattended. In fact, Ken was so frustrated that he wanted to quit and go home.

"It's true Ken did have a bad day," Tom Williams said. "Pass receivers made him look pretty sad. But he was playing tight safety for the first time, and it was an entirely new position for him."

Fortunately, head coach Wally Lemm took the rookie aside and urged him not to get too discouraged too quickly. Ken agreed to stick around, and before long he began to master his new position. "After a week back there in the secondary, he didn't look like the same player," said Williams.

Houston continued to improve during the exhibition season. But when the regular season began, he was put on the bench behind starting strong safety Bobby Jancik. He stayed there for only two games, however. The Oilers' third game was against the San Diego Chargers. Before that game, coach Lemm decided to make use of the 6-foot-3, 198-pound rookie. He feared that the 5-foot-11, 178-pound Jancik would have trouble covering the much bigger, heavier Charger tight ends.

Ken made an impressive showing in that game, and from then on he was the Oilers' starting safety. As the 1967 season progressed, so did Ken. In one game against the Jets, he intercepted four passes, returning two for touchdowns, and ran back a blocked field-goal attempt 71 yards for another score. Thanks in no small measure to their outstanding rookie strong safety, the Oilers leaped to first place in their division with a winning 9–4–1 record.

"Ken has lots of ability and he's going to get better," said defensive coach Walt Schlinkman. "All he needs is the experience. He doesn't make too many mistakes. And when he does, he has the speed and quickness to make up for them. He's big enough to force in end runs, and he's big and fast on pass defense."

"Ken is a real dedicated football player," added general manager Don Klosterman. "He's always trying to improve himself. All during the off-season he would come by the practice field and run two or three times a week. I think it's only a matter of time until he's the best tight safety in football."

Ken continued to improve in the years that followed. But the Oilers didn't do nearly as well. In both 1968 and '69 they lost as many games as they won. And then in 1970 they started a disastrous decline. In the next four years they won only 9 of 56 games.

Ken's outstanding individual play was the only bright spot amidst the gloom, frustration, and constant shuffling in and out of players and coaches that characterize a cellar-dwelling team. Ken had his record-breaking season in 1971, but the Oilers won only four games that year. And Ken's touchdown returns were the deciding factor in three of those victories.

In the spring of 1973 the Washington Redskins offered the Oilers five of their players. All they wanted in return was a sixth-round draft choice—and Ken Houston. It was too good a deal for the downtrodden Oilers to resist, and they reluctantly agreed to the trade.

"When I first heard I'd been traded, naturally the first question was, 'Who was it?' " Houston recalled. "After I heard it was Washington, I was all smiles. You can play there a long time, and coach George Allen takes care of his players. Just about everybody in the league would like to play there. I liked the trade more after I thought about it. I didn't at first. In fact, I didn't think I'd be traded that year. I'd talked contract with Sid Gillman [then the new Oiler general manager] and he'd assured me I wouldn't be traded.

"But I could understand it. He could better his club. We talked after the trade, and I could understand his point of view. There were no hard feelings. Financially, it was a good move. Also, as far as getting a Super Bowl ring, it was a good move. I knew I'd have a chance to be on a winner."

The previous season the Redskins had lost, 14–7, to the Miami Dolphins in the Super Bowl. "A team that's been to the Super Bowl and doesn't win usually goes back again," Houston noted at the time. "I hope they do. Make that I hope *we* do."

Houston had a lot to learn with the Redskins. Under Allen's leadership, they played a wide variety of sophisticated defenses. Brig Owens, Washington's veteran strong safety, was already familiar with Allen's system, so he had a tremendous advantage over Houston, the newcomer.

At the start of the 1973 exhibition season, Houston found himself the league's most expensive benchwarmer. But he didn't complain. He knew it would take time to learn the Redskin way of doing things. "George Allen knows more defense than anybody I ever met," said Houston. "And Brig is playing so well now he'll make All-Pro if he keeps it up.

"I feel I can start, too, and that makes for a stronger club. The fact is, this reminds me of an All-Star team, anyway. In some ways, it's kind of scary here, because you almost know that ten years from now there are going to be eight or nine guys off this team in the Hall of Fame. Someone has to relegate himself to being a good backup, even though I want to play and I want to start."

Houston got his chance to play before the regular

After making an interception against San Diego in a 1973 game, Ken (now a Redskin) heads for the goal post.

season even began. In an exhibition game against Detroit, veteran Redskin free safety Rosey Taylor suffered a fractured elbow. Allen moved Owens to Taylor's spot and put Houston in at strong safety.

"I didn't want it to happen like this," said Ken. "Nobody wants to see a guy go down, even if he's a starter and you're number two. I didn't resign myself to backing up, but I would have. Both of them have been doing a good job. I wasn't even with either one of them because they know the system. I'm still learning."

But Houston was a fast learner, as he showed in his first practice session with the Redskins' starting secondary. After the two-hour workout, defensive backfield coach Ralph Hawkins said, "We had no problems out there today. Ken stepped right in, just like we expected he could do. If Coach Allen hadn't had the foresight to trade for the guy, where would we be now? He gave us depth, and we've got it now when we need it most."

Houston proved that he belonged in the starting line-up in the season's opener. Once again, he picked on the San Diego Chargers. The Redskins routed the Chargers, 38–0, intercepting four passes, recovering three fumbles, sacking quarterback Johnny Unitas five times and his replacement three times, and holding the Charger passing game to an overall seven net yards. Houston was credited with two of the interceptions and one of the fumble recoveries.

"On my first interception we had everybody covered. Unitas had to make an overthrow, and I was in position to catch it," said Houston of a pass he returned 22 yards to the San Diego 15. "The second one was a good ball, and I just beat the receiver to it," Houston continued. He was referring to a fourth-quarter theft that eventually led to the Redskins' final touchdown of the afternoon.

The '73 season was a fine one for the Redskins. They wound up at the top of their division with a 10–4 record. But their hopes for a return engagement at the Super Bowl were soon dashed. In the opening round of the playoffs, they were eliminated by the Minnesota Vikings. The following season was more of the same. Again the 'Skins finished with a 10–4 record. And again they were defeated in the playoffs, this time by the Los Angeles Rams. But no one, it seemed, could defeat Ken Houston. In his first eight years in the league, he earned seven Pro Bowl invitations and a reputation as the best strong safety in the NFL.

Although he was best known for his record-breaking effort of 1971, Houston was proudest of a single play he made early in the 1973 season. In the closing seconds of a hard-fought game against the Dallas Cowboys, the 'Skins were leading 14–7. But the Cowboys had the ball deep in Washington territory and were threatening to tie the game up. On fourth down and goal-to-go, Dallas quarterback Roger Staubach made a last-ditch attempt to close the gap. He zipped the ball to fullback Walt Garrison, who was all alone at the 5-yard line. Garrison, a bull of a man, stormed unimpeded toward the goal line.

It looked like a certain touchdown, but he never made it. Ken Houston came roaring up to meet the 205-pound Garrison head-on at the 1-yard line. He

Houston stops Giant running back Doug Kotar in a 1974 game.

dropped him dead in his tracks. The impact of the tackle stunned the huge Redskin home crowd, and the final gun went off seconds later in eerie silence.

"I have never been hit like that," said Garrison. "I always felt that with a head of steam I could score on anybody hitting me at the one-yard line."

But Ken Houston wasn't just anybody. As one NFL scout put it, "There is no competition among the league's strong safeties. There's Ken Houston and twenty-five others!"

85

LARRY LITTLE

The power sweep is one of the classic plays of football. The key to its success is the ability of the offensive guards to pull out of the line and lead the running back around the corner, knocking down any tacklers they meet along the way. There was no play in the Miami Dolphins' book that All-Pro guard Larry Little enjoyed more. There was no play enjoyed less by opposing cornerbacks, the defenders usually responsible for stopping it.

Stopping Little was no easy task. Nicknamed "Chicken" because of his great appetite for the bird that made Colonel Sanders famous, Little was a barrel of a man. At 6-foot-1 and 265 pounds, he looked fat and slow. But appearances can be deceiving—and they certainly were in Little's case. Just ask the men who have made a living running behind his blocks. Or, better still, revive the undersized, overmatched cornerbacks he's flattened on sweeps and ask them.

Powerful Larry Csonka, the former Dolphin fullback, was Little's number one fan. "When I go out on a sweep behind Little," Csonka said, "I can actually see the fear in those cornerbacks' eyes. Sometimes I grab the back of Little's jersey and just let him pull me through. A guy like that is a real comfort.

"I'll be running behind Chicken, then I'll realize he's pulling away from me. He's so fast for a big fellow that I sometimes actually grab hold of his pants to keep up."

Little, who was once timed at 4.9 seconds for the 40-yard dash (the speed of some NFL backs), chuckled at his ex-teammate's praise and said, "Aw, Csonka overdoes it. Larry is faster than most people think, though I have to admit he has hooked onto my pants a couple of times. Once Csonka was grabbing at me and it caused me to miss my block. I told him to stay close, but not that close.

"You want to keep your feet because you don't want to settle for one block on the sweep," added Little, warming to the subject. "You don't want to cut 'em down. What you want is to run right through them. You want them to know what you did and who it was that did it because you want them to know what's going to happen when you come at them the next time.

"Knocking people down is my business. I've always liked the ferociousness of great blocks. I feel I was gifted with size, strength, and speed. I should use them."

Little used his natural gifts so well that Miami coach Don Shula compared him to former Baltimore Colt guard Jim Parker. A Hall of Fame member, Parker was considered by many to be the greatest guard ever. "They have many of the same traits, although Larry may be faster," said Shula. "Both put fear into corner-backs when they turn upfield on sweeps. Larry can become one of the all-time greats at his position if he keeps working, keeps his weight down, and retains his desire to block people."

Retaining his desire was no problem for Little. To him, pro football was a do-or-die struggle that required intense mental and physical preparation.

"I start really concentrating the afternoon before the game, thinking about what I've got to do," Little explained. "I'll go over the playbook for a while. I think about winning first, then build up the killer instinct in myself. If you don't get that other guy . . . he's gonna get you."

More often than not, it was Little who got the other guy. A perennial All-Star, he was voted the American Football Conference's outstanding offensive lineman for three straight years. As far as Little was concerned, however, that was just the beginning. "Three in a row isn't much," he explained. "Dick Butkus [the former Chicago Bears' star middle linebacker] got something like seven in a row."

Larry Little was obviously an ambitious man. And his greatest ambition was to be elected to football's Hall of Fame. "I don't know what it takes," he said. "And I don't know how many guards are in there. But that's my ultimate personal goal. I've reached every other goal a lineman can reach."

Dolphin guard Larry Little (66) leads a sweep for running back Mercury Morris. The other blocker is Bob Kuechenberg (67).

Little wasn't an overnight success, however. For many years his future in football seemed anything but promising. He was pudgy—no, fat—and seemed more comfortable with a knife and fork than with pads and cleats. In fact, he looked more like a future candidate for the Eating Hall of Fame than like a potential superstar.

Little always loved to eat. He was born in Groveland, Georgia, the second of six children. When Larry was still an infant, his family moved to Miami's black ghetto, and Larry grew up there. His father was a laborer, and his mother did domestic work. Life was hard for the Littles, and they made many sacrifices to keep their children well fed. And even then, filling Larry Little's belly was quite a challenge.

"My mother provided for us but not for herself," he recalled. "She went quite a few years without buying a dress so she could buy for us. We were poor, but I was never hungry. We ate good. I ate more than anybody in the family. Any food anybody didn't want, I was always around to get it. My mother would cook for everybody else, but if they were having something I didn't like, she'd cook for me separate."

The poverty of ghetto life drove many youngsters in Little's neighborhood to crime. But Larry's parents took strong measures to keep him straight. "I never got caught doing anything because I knew what my momma and poppa would do if they found out I was in trouble," Larry admitted. "We always had good close supervision at home, and I'm convinced it kept me out of jail."

Little did get into a bit of trouble once, but his mother made sure it didn't happen again. "Larry and some other boys in the sixth grade were disobedient in school or talked back to the teacher," Mrs. Little recalled, "so they were expelled from Phillis Wheatley Elementary for five days. Although the teacher gave him a note to bring home to us, he didn't. He didn't say a word about it. He thought he could roam the streets for five days and we wouldn't find out.

"The next morning he got up, got dressed, and left the house as if he were going to school. A friend of mine saw him on the street during the time he should have been at school. And she told us that night.

"Larry was at a Boy Scout meeting when I found out. I couldn't wait till he came home, so I went and got him. I gave him the worst punishment he ever got. With a strap. And the next morning we took him to school and made him apologize to the teacher."

In addition to the strap, Larry found another incentive to keep him out of mischief—sports. He played games of tackle football—"no equipment, four, five on a side." Later he played for Miami's Booker T. Washington High School, and still later for Bethune-Cookman, a small black college in nearby Daytona Beach.

Larry entered college weighing 215 pounds. As a sophomore, he weighed 240. As a junior, he weighed 250. And as a senior, he tipped the scales at 260. Larry wasn't the only heavyweight at Bethune-Cookman, however. "We had a 290-pound fullback," Little recalled. "You had to block for him or risk getting stepped on."

At Bethune-Cookman, Little played both offensive and defensive line. In his senior year he was named team captain. He was also named to the All-Southern Intercollegiate Conference team. That was a far cry from making All-America, but then Bethune-Cookman was hardly a major football power.

"I give my college coaches a lot of credit," he said. "We only had two coaches where some schools have ten or twelve. Tank Johnson worked with me until dark many days, and coach Jack McClairen wanted to make me into an outstanding player. McClairen, you know, was the last Bethune-Cookman graduate to make the pros. He was a great tight end for the Pittsburgh Steelers in the fifties."

As graduation approached, Little began paying lots of attention to newspaper and magazine stories about pro football players, especially offensive linemen. "I used to like the Colts, and Jim Parker was my hero," he explained. "He was a fantastic blocker, recognized as the best in the pros. I always wanted to be like him from the days when Parker was an All-America at Ohio State."

In the 1967 college draft, however, Little was ignored by every pro team. Larry was so disappointed that he lost his appetite (temporarily, to be sure). "That is when you know something's bothering me," he laughingly admitted.

Fortunately, a number of teams contacted Little soon after the draft and suggested he try out as a free agent. "The first to contact me was Baltimore," he recalled. "Don Shula was the head coach there then. But I chose

San Diego because they offered me a bonus—the magnificent sum of $750. You can't go very far on that, but it was the biggest amount of money I'd ever seen at one time."

The first thing Little learned about pro football was that a rookie free agent is a second-class citizen. When he got to the Chargers' training camp, he discovered that he and seven other free agents had been asked to report a full week ahead of the drafted rookies. "That really got to my pride," he said. "They were rookies like I was. No reason for me to report a week ahead of them. And the day I arrived there was a newspaper article that said maybe one or two of the free agents might stick around. That kind of got to me."

Little stuck around for two years with the Chargers, but it was not a happy time for him or for then head coach Sid Gillman. Gillman tried threats, jokes, and flattery to get the 273-pound Little to slim down. In desperation, Gillman even put Little in at fullback. That made Larry pretty unhappy—but not unhappy enough to lose his appetite.

"It wasn't for me," Larry recalled. "I don't like to get hit. I'd rather hit. All that running around and running out for passes, people hitting you around your knees, they can have it. I'll take offensive guard."

It was about then that Little got his nickname. After watching him demolish two half-chickens, his Charger teammates started calling him "Chicken." Coach Gillman was not amused, however. By the end of the 1968 season, he concluded that he'd lost the battle of the bulge and that Chicken Little was actually a turkey.

And early in the summer of 1969 Little was traded to the Miami Dolphins for Mack Lamb, an obscure running back.

Little was shocked when he heard about the deal. "I'm bitter," he said at the time. "I didn't see any reason I should be traded. Not that I don't like going to Miami. That's my hometown, and I love it there. But I was doing a lot of playing in San Diego. Still, I guess this is what you have to expect. I spoke to coach Gillman, and he said this is the way pro sports work. You have to expect to be traded somewhere along the line."

A 285-pound Little played with the Dolphins under coach George Wilson for one season. Then Wilson was replaced by former Baltimore coach Don Shula. A stern, no-nonsense man, Shula was determined to get Little back into shape. Little got the message the first time he met Shula, at an introductory banquet for the new coach. "I could see he didn't like all that weight I was carrying," Little said.

Shortly after the banquet Shula made his dissatisfaction even clearer. He told Little that he expected him to slim down to 265 pounds for spring training—and that he'd fine him $10 per pound for anything over that. "I had been expecting 270 or 275, but that 265 level put me in a sweat," Little recalled. "I did a lot of running and passed up some meals."

As the deadline approached, however, Little was still five pounds overweight. Fortunately for him, a players' strike delayed the start of spring training. "Those two weeks we stayed away from camp let me get to 265," Little said, "and I've never been above it since."

His teammates hardly recognized the new trim Little on the first day of training. On the second day of training (which was more rigorous than usual to make up for time lost during the strike) they thought they might have to bury this new trim Little. "I flaked out . . . keeled over," he explained. "Some people thought I had died."

Offensive line coach Monte Clark vividly recalled the incident. "One minute he was standing next to me," said Clark, "and the next minute he had disappeared. Larry was lying on the ground, flat on his back. We had to call a station wagon to haul him away."

"Once Little lost all that weight," said Shula, "he became a part of the real identity of our football team . . . the good, tough running game. I think that was solidified during a Monday night TV game in 1970 against the Falcons at Atlanta. We knew Atlanta was a physical bunch and would try to jam the ball down our throats. Thanks to Larry and the rest of the offense, we jammed it down theirs. Our football team seemed to come of age that night."

The Dolphins had been formed as an expansion team in 1966 and had moved steadily up in the standings every year since then. In 1970 they had their best season yet, finishing with a fine 10–4 record. Much of the credit for Miami's success went to running backs Larry Csonka and Jim Kiick. But the two great runners were the first to admit that they couldn't have run very far without big Larry Little's blocking.

Little and the Dolphins continued to improve, and by 1972 they were as good as a team can get. They wound

Little (66) throws a block against the Baltimore Colts as Larry Csonka tries to bull his way past two defensemen.

Larry romps in the Florida surf with some of the youngsters from his Gold Coast Summer Camp.

up that season with a perfect 14–0 record, then breezed through the playoffs to meet the Washington Redskins in the Super Bowl. There the Dolphins kept up their winning pace to defeat the 'Skins, 14–7, and capture their first league championship.

The 1973 season was another banner year for the Dolphins. After finishing the regular season with a 12–2 record they again went all the way to Super Bowl. This time they defeated the Minnesota Vikings, 24–7, and walked off with their second straight title. Once more, Little played a major role in Miami's victory.

Those were good years for Larry and his teammates. Little wanted to share some of his happiness with others less fortunate than he. So in 1970 he and several other Dolphins founded the Gold Coast Summer Camp for underprivileged children in the Miami area.

Little was delighted with the camp, and so were the youngsters. "The first year we had 'em sleeping in tents down at the end of the beach," he recalled. "But ever since then we've been at Biscayne College in air-conditioned dorms. The kids don't want to go home. They're not used to three square meals and air conditioning.

"It's a football-oriented camp, but we try to teach the kids discipline. We don't stand for any nonsense. Fred Woodson once caught a kid gambling, and he took him home. Another year we caught a kid stealing, but we gave him another chance. The last day, another kid was missing a radio. We found it on the other kid. I told him how much it hurt me, that he'd do this. I tried to show him how stealing can lead to robbery, how robbery can lead to murder. I rap all the time."

Little didn't confine his rapping to the camp, how-ever. He was well known and well liked throughout the entire Miami ghetto. "I'm always around the commu-nity," Little explained. "Sometimes the kids notice the nameplate on my car and wave. I'll stop, and we'll start talking. It isn't something that's planned. I do have my private life, too, you know. I don't just up and say, 'I'm going to be with these kids.' It's an impromptu thing. They know I don't want to be a phony with them. I just want to be like any other normal human being—to get along with people and to have them get along with me."

In recognition of his civic work, Little was awarded an honorary degree as Doctor of Science and Human Relations by Biscayne College. He also received the Whitney M. Young Humanitarian Award from the National Urban League and was proclaimed "King for a Day" by the Miami Variety Children's Hospital.

As popular as he was among the citizens of Miami, the name Larry Little was hardly a household word to most football fans. More often than not, the name Little made them think of Floyd Little, the former Denver Bronco runner. That was hardly surprising. Quarter-backs and running backs have always gotten the lion's share of attention from the public. And offensive linemen have always been football's unsung heroes.

Little never let his lack of fame bother him, though. "I have no choice," he said with a laugh. "I'm a guard. That's what I am. I played this game seventeen years and never once scored a touchdown. Once in college I intercepted a screen pass and ran it for forty yards, but I got tired."

Little could console himself with all the touchdowns his blocks have produced, however. "Chicken's a big truck," Kiick once said. "When he gets rolling on an end sweep, the traffic suddenly thins out. I feel sorry for the little defensive backs coming up on the play. Larry wipes 'em out."

When Chicken Little hits a man, he well might think the sky is falling.

RAY GUY

On a sunny May 1973 afternoon in Oakland, California, Ray Guy made his debut as a professional punter. The long, lanky Raider rookie was working out with his new teammates for the first time. Ray bent at the waist, extended his hands, and waited for the snap—just as he'd done hundreds of times in high school and college. Outwardly, he appeared calm, but that was just an illusion. Inside, he was nervous as can be—and with good reason.

Guy knew he was being watched closely by the other players. Ordinarily, the Raider veterans would have paid little attention to a rookie, especially a kicker. But Ray Guy was not just another rookie, and he certainly wasn't just another kicker. He was the Raiders' number one draft choice, the first NFL kicker ever to be drafted on the first round. Naturally, the Raider vets were curious and no doubt a bit skeptical about Guy. They'd be hard men to impress.

At the snap, Guy swung his leg and kicked the ball. But he was just off the mark. The ball hit the side of his foot, then dribbled a pitiful few yards. Some Raiders groaned softly. Others rolled their eyes. Guy just stood there. "I remember thinking to myself, 'Oh my goodness, there goes my contract,' " he later admitted.

Fortunately for Guy, his next punt spiraled some 65 yards, soaring so high it looked like a brown dot in the cloudless blue sky. Then, as the Raiders watched in amazement, he kicked another, even higher and longer.

Learning that Guy was only 22 years old, defensive back George Atkinson immediately predicted a bright future for the Raiders. "Who knows how far he'll be able to kick in a couple of years!" Atkinson marveled. "The ball seems to take off and then just carry. If he can punt consistently like that, he'll have no trouble and neither will we. If he gets just a little wind behind him, he should be able to kick from end zone to end zone."

A few seconds later, Guy almost did just that. Putting everything he had behind his powerful right foot, he boomed one from the 20-yard line that traveled the length of the field, cleared the opposite goal posts, bounced, rolled, and finally came to rest against a fence some 120 yards away from its starting point.

Jaws dropped. Mouths hung open. The silence surrounding the field was deafening. The first kicker in NFL history to be a number one draft choice had found a home.

The length and height of Guy's towering punts were

just what Oakland had been searching for. With their star-studded line-up, the Raiders could afford the luxury of using their number one draft choice for a great kicker. Hopefully, Guy's super punts would serve as insurance when the Raiders' wide-open, pass-oriented offense failed to get off the ground, leaving them pinned back deep in their own territory.

"We are a gambling team," explained Oakland head coach John Madden. "We need a punter who can get us out of the hole if necessary. We like to throw long, and if we have a punter who can't bail us out, we are really in trouble. If we're running the ball from our own 20, we have to spend three plays trying to pick up the first down. With a good punter, we can gamble and spray the air with passes. If you have Guy around, you can gamble on those three plays, knowing he'll put the ball deep into their territory if you fail."

Guy more than lived up to the Raiders' expectations in the years that followed. He became one of the league's most reliable kickers. Although the distance a punter gets on his kicks is the official measure by which he is judged, the pros are more concerned about the "hang time" of a punt, or the number of seconds the ball stays in the air. The longer the ball stays up, the more time the men covering the punt have to get downfield into position to tackle the returner and prevent a long runback. And no one could hang a punt in the air longer than Guy.

"I think the average hang time in pro football is around 4.5 seconds," Ray said. "My average is between 4.8 and 5 seconds. I've always strived for height.

The Oakland Raiders' Ray Guy was the first kicker ever to be chosen in the first-round of the NFL draft.

Without height, and with those sprint men waiting to run back punts, you'll have the ball right back where you kicked it. Distance comes with height."

The extra half-second Guy managed to keep the ball in the air may not seem like much, but it often meant the difference between no return and a long touchdown runback. "Guy gets great rotation on the ball," said former Green Bay Packer return man Bob Hudson, who came to the Raiders in a trade and had a tough time trying to field Guy's booming practice kicks. "The ball seems to break away from you. If he ever gets a little cross wind, you might never catch the thing."

Kicking an uncatchable ball would be the fulfillment of a lifelong dream for Guy, who always wanted to be a great kicker. "I started behind my house when I was six years old with one of those itty-bitty toy footballs," he recalled. "I've been doing it ever since. I love it."

Guy was the youngest of three football-playing brothers born to D.F. and Annette Guy in Swainsboro, Georgia. Ray's father was a contractor, who moved his family to Athens, then Thomson, then Warrenton, Georgia, three nearby small towns. Ray went to grammar school in all three communities. The Guys finally settled in Thomson because Ray's brother Larry, a fine fullback, wanted to play for Thomson High.

Ray wound up playing for Thomson, too. As a sophomore he averaged 43 yards per punt. In his final two years he increased that to 46, then 49 yards. He also put in some time as quarterback and defensive back, leading his team to back-to-back 12–0 seasons and two state championships.

In the spring, Ray devoted himself to baseball. A fine pitcher, he was drafted by the Cincinnati Reds at the end of his high school career. But instead of signing with the Reds, he accepted a football scholarship to Southern Mississippi.

Guy did everything but sell tickets for the Southern Mississippi football team. In addition to his punts, field goals, extra points, and kickoffs, he also started at safety. During one spring coach P.W. "Bear" Underwood tried him at quarterback. Ray did a terrific job there, too.

"Ray is the greatest kid I ever coached," said Underwood. "I can remember so many pressure situations where he came through for us. He'd intercept three or four passes in a game, get off a ninety-three-yard punt, and then kick a fifty-yard field goal.

"The further back we were pushed toward our end zone, the better was his punting. He got a couple of bad snaps in his senior season, yet he's so fast he was able to run with the ball and pick up a first down in both cases.

"He's a dedicated athlete who works diligently at improving himself. Extra practices don't bother him. He'd do his punting before our regular practice. Then he'd practice with the team for two hours. And then he'd go off by himself, grab a football, call a teammate over, and practice his field-goal kicking.

"He's also a heck of a pitcher. One day he pitched a no-hit, no-run game in the first part of a double-header. Do you know what he was doing during the second game? He was over at the football field practicing his punting."

In his three seasons at Southern Mississippi, Guy finished second, fourth, and first in the nation in punting. His three-year average for 200 punts was 44.7 yards. As a place-kicker, he made 51 of 59 extra-point attempts and 25 of 59 field-goal tries. One of those was an NCAA record 61-yarder, and six others went for more than 40 yards each. On kickoffs, 55 of his 101 efforts sailed into the end zone.

The Raiders were well aware of Guy's eye-popping statistics. And Guy was well aware that in 1972 Oakland's punter, Jerry DePoyster, had ranked last among the league's regular kickers with a 36.9-yard average. Still, it came as quite a surprise when the Raiders made Guy their number one choice in the '73 draft.

"I never heard of a kicker going number one in the draft," said Guy when he heard the news. "A man from the Raiders came down the day before the draft and talked to me at my college. He didn't have any idea at all that I was going to be their number one draft, and I didn't either. One of my friends on the newspaper at school called me and told me I had been drafted number one by Oakland. I couldn't believe it. After I heard it, I had to sit down. I guess I was in shock. I thought I would go in the third or fourth round and to New England. I had heard from the Patriots a lot, but until the man came to see me I had never heard from Oakland."

Ray had heard again from the Cincinnati Reds, however. They had followed his college baseball career and again selected him in the free-agent draft. This time

Guy didn't turn them down so quickly. He happily sat back and let the Raiders and Reds fight it out for his services. "I'm just going to wait and see how the negotiations go," he said while his agent was talking to the Raiders.

The Raiders won the bidding war, and Ray signed with them. Later that summer the Raiders got to observe Guy under the pressure of a big pro rush. In the 1973 College All-Star game, Guy and a squad of other talented rookies took on the defending Super Bowl champion Miami Dolphins. The pros usually romp to victory in this annual charity game, but the Dolphins had to struggle for their 14–3 win. Ray Guy's punts kept them bottled up deep in their own territory for most of the game.

That night Guy averaged 44.1 yards on nine punts, including an initial 55-yarder that was downed on Miami's 2-yard line. He also accounted for the All-Stars' one score with a 37-yard field goal and was voted his team's Most Valuable Player.

"Guy was a real factor in the game," said coach Don Shula of the Dolphins.

"He is the one who hurt us the most," Dolphin running back Jim Kiick added. "He put us in trouble. We never really had good field position except once because of him, and that had to help their defense."

Guy was unimpressed, both by the rush of the Dolphins and his own performance. "The rush was real

Ray gets off a towering punt during a 1973 game.

quick, but it didn't bother me," he said after the game. "I'm used to it. I thought I just had an average night, and I guess I could have kicked better."

Ray did recall one special kick during his college days that was anything but average. "You know the University of California stadium in Berkeley?" he asked. "I kicked one to the top of it during a game. My ball went to the rim of the stadium."

There were plenty of other great kicks from Guy once he joined the Raiders. Yet in the most amazing play of his rookie season, Guy didn't even get his foot on the ball. The Raiders were playing the Pittsburgh Steelers one rainy day. The field was wet and slippery, and so was the ball. Not surprisingly, Guy fumbled the snap. The surprising part came next. As Mean Joe Greene and the rest of the notorious Steeler defenders closed in on him, Guy scooped up the ball and weaved 21 yards downfield for a first down.

Of course, Ray got even better yardage when he stuck to his powerful punting. He finished his first season with an outstanding average of 45.3 yards per punt. The only punter to outdistance him was Kansas City's Jerrel Wilson, a perennial league leader in punting. And Wilson's 45.5-yard average was just inches better than Guy's.

Wilson was considered the game's greatest kicker by most fans and experts. But he was as impressed as anyone with the Raider rookie. "Guy's young, and if he keeps hitting the ball as well as he does now, there's no telling how great he can be," said Wilson. "What makes him such a good kicker is natural timing. He's a tremendous athlete."

Guy himself wasn't quite sure what made his kicks so effective. "I've been trying to find out all these years but I haven't figured it out yet," he said. "I guess you've got to have loose muscles. On some of my kicks I kick my leg so high—six or six and a half feet—it hits the face mask of my helmet. Usually good punters are around 6-foot-1 or 6-foot-2 [Guy was 6-foot-3 and weighed 198 pounds] with long legs. But you find guys who are 5-foot-11 who are real good kickers.

"Where I get most of my power from is what coaches call the whip in your leg. That's when your leg comes up real quick. I've had a lot of people ask me what I do to develop this whip. All I tell them is that I never lifted much weight with my leg, as some people think a kicker should do. It's just something I was born with, and I developed it the best I could."

Raider coaches were wise enough not to tinker with Guy's home-grown methods. "They just told me to kick natural and not try to change anything, so I haven't really learned anything as a pro I didn't know before," he said. "I know that some people will say the more kicking you do, the more tired your leg will get. I don't think that's true. I think the more you kick, the stronger your leg will get. Every day at practice, I'll kick between seventy-five and a hundred balls on kickoffs, and then I'll punt seventy-five to a hundred balls."

The result of all that practice was another great season for Guy in 1974. That year he led all the league's

In a 1975 game against Cincinnati, Ray blasts a 48-yard punt into the end zone . . .

punters with a 42.2-yard average. And he enhanced his value by kicking off for the Raiders.

Most other teams would probably have used Guy for field-goal kicking as well. But the Raiders preferred to save Guy for the punting and bring in a fresh player for the three-pointers. So they used veteran George Blanda for field goals, even though the 47-year-old Blanda was the first to admit that Guy had a far more powerful leg.

"George and I are real good friends," Guy said. "In practice, we go out there together and kick a lot. Not so much field goals. He comes out when I'm doing my kickoffs and kicks with me just to get loose. He and I have a lot of contests to see who can kick the ball the farthest. I have to spot him seven yards, before he'll play with me, though."

. . . **before being blasted by the Bengals, who were then penalized five yards for running into the kicker.**

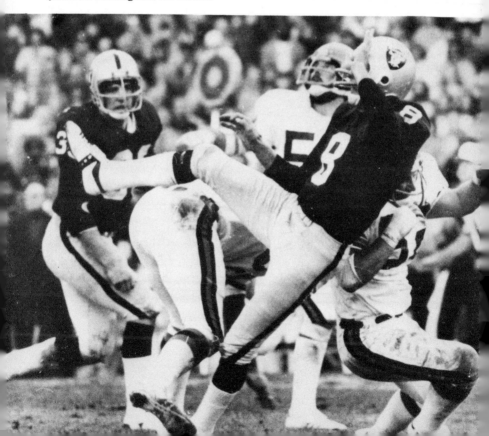

Kicking off and punting kept Guy busy and happy. "The satisfaction for me is knowing that in a close game, the kicking game will often be the determining factor in who wins," he said. "It's very satisfying to me to keep the opposing team in the hole. What I mean by the hole is to keep them inside their twenty-yard line all day. If I can do that, I've helped both my offense and defense."

Guy began the 1975 season in top form. In the opener, against Miami, he showed just how valuable a punter can be. That night Guy averaged 48 yards on six punts. His most conspicuous contribution to the Raiders' 31–21 victory was a 69-yard missile he launched from inside his own 10-yard line. After the game Dolphin coach Don Shula said, "There is only one reason Oakland beat us—Ray Guy. His punting kept us in the hole all day long."

Ray's punting kept most of the Raiders' rivals in the hole that season. Oakland finished up with an 11–3 record, and Guy was again the league's best punter. This time he averaged 43.8 yards per kick.

Guy had another outstanding statistic. Through the 1975 season, his third as a pro, not a single one of his kicks had ever been blocked. Guy got his punts off so quickly that opposing defenders couldn't touch him—or the ball.

"It takes me about 2 seconds to get the ball off," Guy explained. "The average punter takes between 2.5 and 3 seconds. What causes that is taking more steps to kick the ball than I do. I take two and a half steps. The average punter takes three or four."

A punter is all alone when he performs his specialty. He has only those few precious seconds to do his thing. If he blows it by dropping the snap, or dribbling the ball 15 yards off the side of his foot, or allowing the ball to be blocked, he has no one to blame but himself.

Most punters feel the pressure, and Guy was no exception. "But I try not to think negative thoughts," he said. "I just concentrate on getting the ball as far away from my end zone as I can. You'd better make a good kick. You've only got one chance, unlike most other players. If you kick it bad, you might as well just keep going . . . right away from everyone."

Fortunately, Ray Guy almost always kicked it well. And it was the ball, not he, that kept going . . . right away from everyone!

ISAAC CURTIS

The Houston Oilers were working on their midweek team drills in preparation for a Sunday visit by the Cincinnati Bengals in early October 1975. In team drills, the offensive starters work against the defensive starters, and each unit takes turns imitating its upcoming opponents' style of play.

A spectator took a quick glance at the Oiler offense as it imitated the attack of the Bengals and did a double take. Every Oiler wide receiver was wearing the same number on his uniform—85. That was Houston coach Bum Phillips's not-so-subtle reminder to his men that the wide receiver who'd be wearing number 85 for the Bengals was the man they would have to stop. And that man was the fleet 6-foot-1, 193-pound Isaac Curtis.

The Oiler defensive backs hardly needed the reminder. "Curtis runs a 9.1; no, make that 9.2," said

Houston cornerback Willie Alexander. "Aw, what's the difference. You can't run with him. All you can do is try to cut him off. But one mistake, one false step, and it's a touchdown."

By the end of the 1975 season, his third in the NFL, Isaac Curtis had caught 119 passes for 2,410 yards and 26 touchdowns. That works out to an average of 20.2 yards per catch and a touchdown for every 4.5 receptions, dramatic statistical proof that Isaac Curtis was a dangerous man on the loose.

The Oilers weren't the only players to pay special attention to Curtis. The Bengals' opponents consistently double- and triple-teamed the speedy receiver. To slow him down they also used a "bump and run" defense, knocking him down at the line of scrimmage and continuing to knock him down as he tried to run his pass patterns.

In April 1974, however, the "bump and run" was declared illegal. A new NFL rule prohibited defenders from tackling a receiver more than one time per play. The rule was instigated largely by Cincinnati general manager and head coach Paul Brown. It became known as "The Isaac Curtis Rule" because it was obviously designed to free speedsters such as Curtis to run their pass patterns. But it was also a sign of the respect Curtis earned in the NFL that his name—out of those of all the fine wide receivers—became attached to the new rule.

When Isaac Curtis was a boy growing up in Santa Ana, California, he reached the conclusion that he would someday make his mark in sports. The only question in his mind was which sport. At first, he dreamed of becoming "the greatest athlete in the whole wide world." But then he narrowed his sights and decided to concentrate on baseball.

"I wanted to be a baseball star," he recalled with a smile. "Man, when I was a little boy, I dug playing baseball. I think I still hold the Little League record for home runs at San Salvador Park in Santa Ana."

Isaac enjoyed any activity that allowed him to take off, stretch out his long legs, and move into high gear. "I have always liked to run," he explained. "I think everyone enjoys running, no matter how fast they run."

A standout in track and California Player of the Year as a football running back in high school, Curtis was heavily recruited by colleges. He chose the University of California at Berkeley in the San Francisco Bay area because he loved the beauty of the surrounding countryside.

Curtis played freshman football as a running back in the fall of 1969. When spring came, he ran for the track team, leading Cal to the NCAA championship. He finished second in the 100-yard dash, was fourth in the 220, and ran the second leg on Cal's winning 440-yard relay team. Altogether, he accounted for 22 of Cal's team total of 40 points.

In the fall of 1970, Curtis was about to embark on a varsity football career as a runner and kick-return specialist, when he became involved in a controversy that would mar the rest of his career at Cal. It was discovered that Curtis had enrolled at Cal without taking a required entrance exam. "Nobody ever told me

Bengal wide receiver Isaac Curtis was a constant victim of the "bump and run" defense until it was banned by the NFL in 1974.

anything about taking that test," Curtis said. "I had no idea I was even supposed to take one, and no one in the athletic department ever told me I needed to take it."

The NCAA took away the track title Cal had won, thanks largely to Curtis, and ruled him ineligible for further competition. Cal officials protested that Curtis's failure to take the test was due to a clerical error. Therefore, they defied the NCAA's ruling and allowed Curtis to play football in 1970 and '71. The NCAA retaliated by putting the school on probation, banning the whole football team from the Rose Bowl.

Although he continued to play, Curtis was unhappy.

"I try not to think about it any more," he said recently. "At the time, I was bitter. I didn't feel I'd done anything wrong, but there was nothing I could do about any of it."

At the end of his junior year, however, Curtis did do something about the situation. He decided to transfer to San Diego State and play football for coach Don Coryell's pass-happy Aztecs. He also decided to switch his position from running back to pass receiver.

"I wasn't gonna go anywhere at Cal," he explained. "The football program by then was so disorganized. I didn't want to play running back any more because I saw no future in it. I've always felt my natural position was wide receiver. I also felt I'd go higher in the draft as a pass receiver than as a runner. I looked at coach Coryell's program before I went down there, and I was impressed with what he'd done and the kind of person he was. He was honest with me. He told me that if I worked hard, I could become a pro receiver."

Coryell, who later became head coach of the St. Louis Cardinals, immediately began to teach his new player the fine points of pass receiving. "He said that if you didn't run precise patterns, you were wasting steps that you could be using to your advantage," Curtis recalled. "I had never worked a whole lot on footwork before, but he made me realize how important things like that were."

Aztec quarterback Jesse Freitas, who went on to star with the San Diego Chargers, recalled the day Curtis reported for his first spring practice session in 1972. "A lot of pro scouts had come out to the field to time us in the 40-yard dash," said Freitas, "and Curtis ran the 40 in 4.4. But even though he was really fast, it took him a little time to make the changeover. He had played only running back at Cal. During the summer, all the quarterbacks worked with him as he tried to change to a receiver."

By the time the 1972 season ended, there was no denying that Curtis was a receiver—and a fine one, too. In a game against Oregon State, San Diego's major rival, he caught a 70-yard touchdown pass. And in the last game of the season, against Iowa State, he leaped high in the air to grab the 35-yard touchdown pass that won the game.

San Diego wound up with an excellent 10–1 record, and Curtis finished with 44 receptions for 832 yards (18.9 yards per catch) and nine touchdowns. Curtis was picked in the first round of the 1973 NFL draft by the Cincinnati Bengals. "It was between Isaac and Arizona State's Steve Holden," recalled Bengal coach Paul Brown. "We went with Isaac on his pure foot speed. He was the top-rated athlete available on our list when our turn came to choose."

Curtis was flattered to find himself chosen in the first round. "I can't say I was expecting it," he said. "But I was hoping for it. You can't help feeling good over something like that."

The Bengals couldn't help feeling good either when they saw their rookie turn on the speed in one of his first workouts with the team. Dressed in bright red sweat pants, Curtis gracefully sped downfield, snatching one pass after another out of the sky. The normally dour

Brown gleefully observed, "See how those quarterbacks look for those red pants? They already know who he is."

Then Brown continued in an even more uncharacteristic display of enthusiasm. "Isaac is so quick," he raved. "Has he got hands! He's cut from the Paul Warfield mold, only bigger. He's rangy, he has tremendous speed, and he's a nationally known sprinter. When he turns it on . . . eeeeee! It's just something to have, and something we haven't had. He'll be projected into the starting line-up as fast as we can get him in there. Of all the rookies out there—and there are some good ones—he stands out."

Although Curtis pulled a hamstring muscle on the third day of training camp and was sidelined for most of the pre-season, he got into the Bengal's starting line-up a lot faster than he or even Brown expected. Injuries to veteran receivers Chip Myers and Charley Joiner forced Brown to insert Curtis into a starting position in the 1973 regular-season opener against the Denver Broncos.

It figured to be a tough spot for a rookie, but a lack of self-confidence had never been one of Curtis's problems. Asked his long-range goal as he was about to make his pro debut, Curtis declared, "I'd like to be the greatest ever."

Curtis wasn't quite so confident after the game, however. The Bengals took a 28–10 drubbing by the Broncos, and the rookie receiver was unable to help his team. And it took Curtis and third-year quarterback Ken Anderson a few more games to get their act together.

"It wasn't until the fourth or fifth regular-season

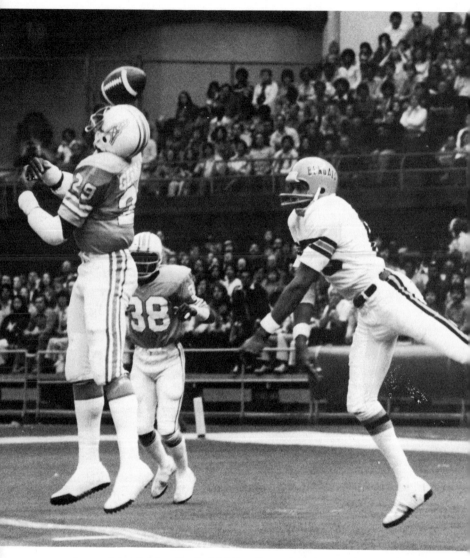

A pass intended for Curtis (right) sails straight into the arms of Houston strong safety Willie Germany.

game that Kenny and I were really satisfied we'd gotten our timing straight," Curtis explained. "In the first couple of games, he was either underthrowing or overthrowing me. But things worked out for us. By the end of the year we were going great.

"To be honest, I didn't find switching to professional football to be that much of an adjustment. It was a lot like going from high school to college. The competition was better because the people were bigger and faster and more talented, but so was I.

"I had heard a lot of stories about how much tougher the pros were going to be than the guys in college, but I don't think I was awed at all. I looked at it like this: the same guys who were ahead of me in high school were waiting for me in college, and the same guys ahead of me in college were waiting for me in the pros."

Curtis got better and better as his rookie season progressed. He wound up catching 45 passes for 843 yards and nine touchdowns and was voted the American Football Conference's Offensive Rookie of the Year. Five of his touchdown receptions came in the Bengals' last two games, victories over the Cleveland Browns and the Houston Oilers.

The Anderson-to-Curtis combination struck early against the Browns. In the first quarter the Bengals had the ball on Cleveland's 9-yard line on a third-and-4 situation. "I ran my shake pattern," Curtis later recalled. "When you're down that close and you fake the cornerback in, well, you're one-on-one with the safety." The safety was all-star Clarence Scott. It didn't matter. Easy touchdown.

Early in the second quarter, Cleveland made a similar mistake. "We were in a slot formation and they matched me up one-on-one with the safety, which is a high-percentage risk," explained Curtis. When he saw that, Anderson did the obvious thing. "I threw the ball up there and let Isaac run to it," the quarterback said. "He just blows by people." Seventy yards later, it was 14–3 in favor of the Bengals.

Finally, with 36 seconds left in the first half, Curtis ran a cross pattern. "They went into a zone and I got down five yards and out across the field." The pass was there. So was Isaac. The 20-yard touchdown made it 21–3, and the Bengals went on to an easy 34–17 victory.

The following week, Curtis grabbed 67- and 77-yard touchdown bombs from Anderson in a hard-fought 27–24 win over the Oilers that clinched Cincinnati's first divisional title. Paul Brown attributed the victory directly to Curtis. "We won the game on a great performance by a super athlete," said the Bengal coach.

The Bengals met the Miami Dolphins in the first round of the playoffs. The Dolphins knew who they had to stop to win—and they knew just how to stop him. Employing the "bump and run" with a vengeance, they completely nullified Curtis and routed the Bengals, 34–16. The brutally effective manner in which the Dolphin defenders continually knocked Curtis down was a major factor in the NFL's decision to ban the "bump and run" in 1974.

"The Dolphins did what other teams had been doing, only they did it better," Curtis said after the game. "The linebacker and defensive back jammed me as I came off the line. Sometimes they tried to hit me low to slow down my legs. But everything they did was more effective than anyone else who had tried it."

In the opening game of the 1974 season, however, Curtis was simply unstoppable. Again the poor Browns were his victims. This time Cleveland took an early 7–0 lead. But with only nine seconds remaining in the first half, Curtis caught a long pass from Anderson and went out of bounds on the Browns' 1-yard line. The Bengals scored on the next play and ended the half with a 7–7 tie. Early in the third period Curtis broke the tie with a 19-yard scoring strike. Then the Bengals went on the rampage, running away with a 33–7 victory.

Although his touchdown reception put them ahead for good, the Bengals all felt that Curtis's catch at the end of the second quarter (the one that set up the tying score) was the key to their victory. "In all pro games, it takes a while to find out who is going to have the momentum," explained Paul Brown after the game. "And for a while today it was difficult to determine who would control the game.

"Curtis's catch really gave us a tremendous boost. I always tell Kenny to make his throws too long when he goes to Isaac. With his speed, he can run under them."

After that fine opening-game effort, Curtis found the rest of the season tough going. For now, in his second year as a pro, Curtis was no longer a rookie surprising opponents with the skills and poise of a veteran. Now he was a marked man—one who was constantly double- and triple-teamed by his rivals. And now that his opponents could no longer legally play "bump and run"

Surrounded by Oilers, Curtis leaps up to snare a pass during a 1975 game.

against him, many took to illegally playing "slug and run."

"Defensive backs have been slugging me all year," said Curtis. "But the referees have called it only once. That was on Kenny Houston of Washington, and he got away with it the entire game before they called it. I never had this problem last year. I've got to take it to a degree, but I'm not going to stand out there like a punching bag."

Curtis also had his share of verbal abuse from frustrated defensemen. "You've always got guys telling you they're going to break your bones," he said. "Some tell you they're never going to let you catch another pass against them."

Of course, with opposing defenses concentrating on Curtis, the other Bengal receivers got free more often. So in a way, Curtis was contributing merely by stepping onto the field. A team player, he was at first content with his decoy role. "As long as the ball is advanced, I don't care how it's done," he said. "They throw the ball to me when they can get the ball to me."

But by the end of the year, the Bengals hardly ever managed to get the ball to Curtis. Injuries to offensive tackle Vern Holland, center Bob Johnson, and running backs Boobie Clark and Essex Johnson caused a breakdown in Bengal pass blocking. Without proper protection, Anderson simply didn't have the time to get the ball to his most dangerous receiver. In the last three games of the season, Curtis caught only one pass, a 24-yarder against the Detroit Lions. The Bengals finished the season with a disappointing 7–7 record and failed to make the playoffs. Despite his difficulties, Curtis finished with a 21.1-yard-per-catch average and ten touchdowns. His total receptions, however, dropped to 30.

During the 1975 training camp period, the Bengals worked hard and long on improving their ability to get the ball to Curtis. The injured Bengal blockers were back in shape, so Anderson would have the kind of protection he needed. Most important, Bill Walsh, the quarterback-receiver coach, suggested that Anderson make a greater effort to reach Curtis.

"Ken has a tendency to give up on Isaac too fast when it's obvious a zone defense is rolling up on him," said Walsh. "This year we're stressing that Ken stay with Isaac until the play develops further."

Curtis could hardly wait for the season to start. "I'm already way ahead of where I was at the end of the '74 season," he said. "It's easier to avoid defenders, read defenses, and adjust my patterns. Experience has made things much easier. Speed is great to have, but you can't live on it forever. Kenny and I can solve any zone if he has time. That was something he wasn't getting toward the end of last season."

The 1975 season turned out to be another fine one for Curtis. He finished with 44 catches for 934 yards (a league-leading 21.2-yard average) and seven touchdowns.

The young boy who had dreamed of becoming "the greatest athlete in the whole world" hadn't been far off the mark. After three years in the NFL, Isaac Curtis was probably the world's greatest wide receiver.

JOE GREENE

Nature has a wide range of frightening phenomena: hurricanes, tornadoes, earthquakes, tidal waves—and Mean Joe Greene when he's lost his temper.

The Pittsburgh Steelers' 6-foot-4, 270-pound left tackle was one of the finest defensive linemen to ever play pro football. A perennial All-Pro selection, Greene combined great size and strength with amazing quickness and a fiercely competitive nature. To top it off, he had an explosive temper that frightened the biggest and baddest players in the NFL.

A Minnesota Viking scouting report on the Steelers once included the notation: "Don't make Joe Greene angry."

The Viking players laughed but were instantly cut off by head coach Bud Grant. "I'm serious," Grant snapped. "Help him up after a play, pat him on the backside, talk to him. Keep him happy. Because if you get him angry, Mean Joe Greene is liable to hurt somebody."

Grant knew what he was talking about. In Joe's rookie year the big tackle was thrown out of 2 of the Steelers' 14 games. The first ejection was for kicking Viking guard Jim Vellone. The other was for a very late—and very painful—hit on Fran Tarkenton, who was then the quarterback of the New York Giants.

And then there was the time Joe shattered several teeth in the mouth of Cleveland Brown center Bob DeMarco; the time he smashed his own helmet by throwing it at the goal post; and the time he admittedly tried to twist an opponent's head off.

Occasionally, Greene declared war on an entire team. Pittsburgh linebacker Andy Russell recalled a time when the Oakland Raiders offended Joe by putting grease on their shoulder pads. "Joe got so angry he could have beaten the Raiders all by himself that day," said Russell.

Russell also witnessed another of Greene's great outbursts. That day the Steelers were playing the Philadelphia Eagles—and losing badly. The Eagles were constantly holding Greene, which angered him a lot. And the refs weren't calling it, which just infuriated him. So Joe decided to take matters into his own huge hands. He snatched the ball away from the startled Eagles' center, heaved it into the second tier of stands, and stomped off the field.

Russell described the moment with awe. "Everybody looked at him," said Russell. " 'He can't be doing this,' we thought. We watched the ball spiral into the seats. It seemed like it took forever. The crowd was dead silent. And the players—there we were, we didn't have a ball, and we didn't have a left tackle. It was like he was saying, 'O.K., if you won't play right, we won't play at all.' Nobody else would do such a thing. In the NFL! Anybody else would get in trouble with the league, with the coaches. Joe did it. In a moment the crowd exploded. They loved it."

Don't get the wrong idea, though. Most of the time, Joe Greene played the game the same way everyone else did—only better. When he joined the Steelers as their number one draft choice in 1969, they had just concluded a 2–11–1 season, their fifth consecutive losing year. By 1975, sparked by a Greene-led "Steel Curtain" defense, they won their first Super Bowl. Constant temper tantrums don't get results like that.

Mean Joe insisted that he wasn't really mean. He explained that his nickname came from his North Texas State College team, which was called The Mean Green. Mean? "It's not me," he said. "I don't hate anybody. I'm loose and easy-going. I'm not a showboat, and I'm not an ogre. I play my best when I'm loose, when I'm laughing. When I get tense or angry, I can't play my best. You forget to concentrate when you do that. . . .

"The thing I don't like about 'Mean' is the image it conjures up. It brings to people's minds something subhuman. I'm very human. I bleed, cry, feed the babies, read. That's the thing I'm paranoid about, that label—'Mean.' Of course, I know it helps me, too. I'm not foolish. Nobodies don't get nicknames."

Joe was always an emotional person. Born and raised in Temple, Texas, he became hooked on football at the age of 12 after watching the Baltimore Colts' famous sudden-death victory over the Giants for the 1958 NFL championship. When he got to high school, Joe played tackle and middle linebacker for the varsity. Even then, he was big, he was good—and he was mean.

"I got a reputation for being the dirtiest ballplayer that ever came out of that area," he admitted. "When we were losing, I'd act the fool. I didn't do that in college because we won. I've never acted crazy in the pros unless we were losing.

"In my sophomore year in high school I got kicked out of nine games. No, I got kicked out of all of 'em. My junior year it was nine.

"I'll tell you how crazy I used to be. A team came to Temple and beat us. We had this little diner in town. I went in there after the game, and the other team was eating. Their quarterback had an ice cream cone. I took it away from him and smeared it all over his face. He didn't do anything. He went back to the team bus. Then I heard somebody call my name. I turned around, and a soda bottle hit my chest. The guy who threw it ducked back into the bus. Like a fool, I went at the bus. In the front door. They all went out the back door."

Because he played for a poorly publicized all-black high school, Greene's reputation for toughness spread no further than the nearby University of Houston. The day Joe was invited to visit the campus turned out to be the same day his high school senior prom was being held. Joe didn't hesitate for a moment. He went to the prom.

Pittsburgh tackle Mean Joe Greene led the Steelers to their first Super Bowl victory.

Fortunately, North Texas State heard about Joe from a local alumnus and offered him a scholarship, which he accepted. In his sophomore year Joe was switched to defensive tackle and had a super season. At the start of the next season, Rod Rust became North Texas's new head coach. "I found out about Joe that day I took the job," said Rust. "Everyone told me I was going to have the best defensive lineman in the country for two years."

As soon as Rust saw Greene in action, he knew the reports were true. "He was always capable of making the big play," Rust recalled. "We knew he'd make a great pro."

In Greene's three varsity years, the North Texas State Eagles racked up a 23–5–1 record. Much of the credit for their success belonged to Joe. He was named an All-America, his uniform number (75) was retired by the school, and the citizens of Temple honored him with a special "Joe Greene Day" celebration.

Greene may have been the toast of Temple, but he was hardly a national figure. In fact, when the Steelers made him their number one draft choice in 1969, the reaction across the country was, "Joe who?" In one newspaper poll, only 3 of 20 Steeler fans interviewed recognized his name.

Joe made his presence known in Pittsburgh almost immediately, however. He got involved in a long, highly publicized salary dispute with the Steelers. It wasn't resolved until 23 days after the rookies' training camp began. At one point Joe threatened to play semi-pro ball for ten dollars a game if he and Pittsburgh couldn't come to terms.

"I was very unhappy about going to the Steelers," Greene explained. "I wanted to go to a winning team. Since I'm from Texas, I knew most about the Dallas Cowboys. I was hoping I could play for them."

When Greene finally showed up at the Pittsburgh training camp, the Steeler veterans were eager to teach the presumptuous rookie a lesson. But it was the veterans who looked like novices when matched against the size, speed, and toughness of Greene. "After a couple of days, we wished we'd never seen him," center Ray Mansfield admitted.

Mansfield was once asked if it was infuriating to go

up against a man who could beat him at will. And Mansfield, one of the toughest blockers in the NFL, replied, "Infuriating? When Joe Greene stomps you, it's not infuriating. It's more like frightening. If Joe really wants to shuck a guy . . . did you ever see a dog get hold of a snake?"

If Joe Greene was frightening in pre-season practice, he was an absolute terror in the regular-season opener against the Cleveland Browns. Although the Browns defeated the Steelers, 42–31, Joe made them pay for every point.

On one play, Greene put a tremendous rush on Cleveland quarterback Bill Nelsen and forced him to throw an interception. Joe instantly switched to offense and took off to block Nelsen. Fortunately for the Nelsen family, Bill reached the sidelines safely before Greene caught up with him. "I saw him coming, and I decided I better get out of there," Nelsen recalled with a shudder. "I was asking myself, 'What's he after me for?' "

Another Brown player, receiver Gary Collins, said, "There they were losing by twenty points, and Greene's laughing and running around all over the place making tackles. What a brute."

"He's gonna be great," said Cleveland guard Gene Hickerson, the man with the unfortunate task of trying to block Greene. "He's strong as a bull and so blasted quick. I don't know how anybody's going to handle him in a year or two. Believe me, I don't know how you handle him right now. Just between you and me, Greene's the best tackle I've seen all year."

That first game set the tone for the rest of the season. The Steelers lost one game after another and wound up with an embarrassing 1–13 record. But no one could deny that Joe was a winner. Steve Van Buren, a former All-Star quarterback proclaimed Greene the greatest tackle he'd ever seen—rookie or veteran. "If he learns anything more," said Van Buren, "he'll kill somebody."

Although Joe was a runaway choice as NFL Defensive Rookie of the Year, it wasn't a happy season for him. "We lost more games in a month than we lost in my four years in college," he said. "That first year was a nightmare. By late October, I was counting the days before I could go home."

When the 1970 season began, however, Joe looked forward to better days. "We got some new players, and I started to be hopeful," he recalled. "By then I really wanted to play in Pittsburgh. I figured it would mean much more to me to be part of building a championship team where there had never been one than to win a championship with a team like the Green Bay Packers, where I would be just another part in the machine."

The Steelers finished the 1970 season with a 5–9 record. That wasn't anything to brag about, but it was a definite improvement. In 1971 they climbed to 6–8. And the following year was their best yet. Pittsburgh got off to a fast start in 1972 and kept up the pace with a steady stream of victories. Joe seemed to get better and better each week. His most outstanding performances came in the last two games of the season.

The Steelers defeated the Houston Oilers, 9–3, in

their next-to-last game of the season. That afternoon
Joe blocked one field-goal try, forced and recovered a
key fumble, sacked quarterback Dan Pastorini five
times, and made six other solo tackles. Not surprisingly,
Greene was named the Associated Press's Defensive
Player of the Week and was awarded the Steelers' game
ball.

**For the fifth time in a single game, Joe sacks quarterback Dan Pastorini of
the Houston Oilers.**

The following Sunday in Pittsburgh, the Steelers took on the San Diego Chargers. At stake was the 1972 American Football Conference's Central Division title. A victory in this game would clinch it for the Steelers. And Joe was determined to get that victory. Three times in the game's final five minutes, the Steelers preserved their slim 21–17 lead by stopping the Chargers inside their own 10-yard line. Each time, it was Greene who put the steel in the Steeler defense.

The first time San Diego had a first down and goal to go from the Steeler 7. The Chargers' rookie running back, Leon Burns, hurled his 230 pounds at the center of the Steeler line. Greene slammed him down after only a yard gain. Then San Diego quarterback John Hadl went to the air twice. And twice he failed to hit his receivers in the end zone. On fourth down he tried again, but the pass never got beyond the line of scrimmage. With an agility and grace that belied his great bulk, Greene leaped and batted the ball harmlessly to the ground.

The next time they got the ball the Chargers drove to Pittsburgh's 10. Hadl faded to throw, but Greene hit him just as he released the pass. The ball fluttered down into the hands of Pittsburgh linebacker Jack Ham.

With only 1:06 left to play, Pittsburgh quarterback Terry Bradshaw fumbled, and San Diego recovered on the Steeler 20. The Chargers made a first down on the 2-yard line, where they called their final time-out.

After selecting their plays, the Chargers came up to the line of scrimmage. Burns hit the middle, but Greene and a host of teammates stopped him for no gain. Burns

Joe gets set to bring down quarterback Dave Hampton in a game against the Green Bay Packers.

tried again. This time Greene dropped him for a one-yard loss.

Bedlam enveloped Three Rivers Stadium as the final seconds ticked away. The officials had to grant Hadl an extra time-out because his signals could not be heard above the roar of the crowd. Hadl had tested Joe Greene all he cared to. On the final play of the game he fired into the end zone, and Jack Ham knocked the ball down. The Steelers' victory gave them a super 11–3 record for the season and clinched their division championship. After 40 years in the NFL, Pittsburgh had its first title of any kind.

As if making up for all those lost years, the Steelers tied for the AFC Central title in the 1973 season and won it outright the following two years. In January 1975 they captured pro football's greatest prize, defeating the Oakland Raiders in the playoffs and the Minnesota Vikings in Super Bowl IX.

Greene was a key factor in the Steelers' march to the Super Bowl. He and his teammates almost completely shut off the running game of the Raiders and Vikings. Using a new defense designed especially to make the most of Greene's great speed, the Steelers held Oakland and Minnesota to a total of only 46 yards rushing on 42 running plays.

"I don't think any teams will copy it," said Pittsburgh coach Chuck Noll of his new defense. "The only reason we could do what we did was Joe Greene. And no one else has Joe Greene. In these playoffs, he has been the greatest defensive lineman I have ever seen. I don't think anyone has ever played greater than he has."

Some people claimed that winning the Super Bowl might make Joe Greene lose the emotional head of steam that had made him the game's finest tackle. But those people didn't know Joe Greene.

"Winning the Super Bowl was everything that I thought it would be," he said in the summer of 1975. "But it's all over so quickly. I mean right now, it's over. We're here in camp, and we're starting all over again fresh. That Super Bowl we won last year doesn't mean a thing for this year. . . . I get mad when people say that we might be complacent, that we're not hungry any more.

"You win one Super Bowl, and where do you go from there? Well, if you're a football player you go on playing to win. They talk about us having to worry about other teams looking for us now. What a bunch of bull! There are twenty-six teams playing football, and they're always looking to beat you."

Every team in the NFL was looking to beat Pittsburgh in 1975. But that didn't stop Joe and the Steelers. They outplayed their competition to finish with a 12–2 record and another division championship. Then they roared through the playoffs and won their second Super Bowl in a row, defeating the Dallas Cowboys, 21–17.

This time few people suggested that Greene might lose his desire to win still another championship. They didn't want to get him angry. For as Viking coach Bud Grant had already noted, ". . . if you get him angry, Mean Joe Greene is liable to hurt somebody."

INDEX

INDEX

150